THE SEPTEMBER-11 CODE

So engrossing was William Downie's d it in one sitting, utterly unable

Downie not only has an ama. with the talent and ease of the s ___ ___ to conceptualize the Code in a way ___ ___ tacinating and easily grasped by the layman, while at the same time providing more than enough mathematical evidence with scriptural types and shadows, to satisfy the biblical scholar and mystic.

With 9/11 so engrained in the global conciousness, *The Secret Code* will appeal to a broad spectrum of readers across all genres. In fact, I predict it will become a modern classic in a genre of its own.

William Downie's book has come forward at a time in history when we are witnessing an increase in spiritual hunger and curiosity across the globe. We've seen books such as *The Da Vinci Code*, a blend of fact and fiction, soar to the Top Seller's list with its blend of mysticism, drama and ancient mystery. How much more so will *The Secret Code* appeal, with the factual and amazing account of a secret code in the bible, unlocked by a mysterious key, which deciphers one of the most earth shattering events of modern history! Regardless of whether one arrives at the same conclusions as the author, the Code itself and the manner in which it was revealed will both intrigue and confound the reader. **Kathryn LeCorre**, Canadian Author

What William Downie has done in this awe inspiring book is nothing short of miraculous. His diligent approach to decoding aspects of the Holy Bible (New International Version) is both thought provoking and astonishing. The author leads the reader into looking at certain aspects of man's inhumanity to man of which the tragic events of the Twin Towers is but one example. His mathematical approach at deducing numbers throughout certain movies and the implications to his overall thesis is also jaw dropping. All in all this is one book that should be read by believers and sceptics alike and upon doing so; you'll most certainly see the world in a different light.

Malcolm Robinson (Founder Strange Phenomena Investigations) Author *UFO Case Files of Scotland* (Volume 1 & 2) and *Paranormal Case Files of Great Britain* (Volume 1)

Many supposed 'codes' have been discovered in recent years, but never one so vital, fascinating and revealing as this. Bill Downie demonstrates that the real secrets affecting the future of humanity and the planet itself lie waiting to be discovered in scripture. This information, which was discovered using the ancient science of gematria, also implies that the very language we speak is a construct founded on mathematical principles and if that does not amaze you then nothing will.

Brian Allen, author of *Dark Messiah, The View From the Abyss, The Hole in the Sky*

The
September-11 Code

The Most Enlightening Revelations
in 2000 Years

The
September-11 Code

The Most Enlightening Revelations
in 2000 Years

William Downie

AXIS MUNDI
BOOKS

Winchester, UK
Washington, USA

First published by Axis Mundi Books, 2012
Axis Mundi Books is an imprint of John Hunt Publishing Ltd., Laurel House, Station Approach,
Alresford, Hants, SO24 9JH, UK
office1@o-books.net
www.o-books.com

For distributor details and how to order please visit the 'Ordering' section on our website.

Text copyright: William Downie 2011

ISBN: 978 1 78099 201 3

A CIP catalogue record for this book is available from the British Library.

Scripture quotations taken from the HOLY BIBLE, NEW INTERNATIONAL VERSION
Copyright © 1973, 1978, 1984 by International Bible Society
Used by permission of Hodder & Stoughton,
a division of Hodder Headline Ltd.
All rights reserved.
'NIV' is a registered trademark of International Bible Society.
UK trademark number 1448790

Design: Stuart Davies

Printed in the USA by Edwards Brothers Malloy

We operate a distinctive and ethical publishing philosophy in all
areas of our business, from our global network of authors to
production and worldwide distribution.

CONTENTS

This work is dedicated to my wife, my daughters,
my grandsons and an unknown woman

The folly of Interpreters has been to foretell times and things by this Prophecy, as if God designed to make them Prophets. By this rashness they have not only exposed themselves, but brought the Prophecy also into contempt. The design of God was much otherwise. He gave this and the Prophecies of the Old Testament, not to gratify men's curiosities by enabling them to foreknow things, but that after they were fulfilled they might be interpreted by the event, and his own Providence, not the Interpreters, be then manifested thereby to the world.

Isaac Newton, *Observations upon the Apocalypse of St. John*

For as lightning that comes from the east is visible even in the west, so will be the coming of the Son of Man.

Matthew 24.27,

Prologue

I always wanted to find buried treasure. In my imagination I would spot something glinting in the sun on a newly ploughed field and discover a bag of gold coins, or maybe a chest laden with jewelry. In reality, of course, I never expected such a find ever to come my way. Yet in a manner of speaking my fantasy came true. Moreover, the discovery I made was far more spectacular than anything I could have dreamed up. However, the treasure I unearthed lay not in any natural soil but in the artificial loam deposited by thousands of years of human culture. And it was hidden, not in the sense of a pirate burying his loot, but in the spirit of a loving father secretly preparing a gift for a child who has come of age.

This book is the improbable yet absolutely true story of my treasure hunt, along with an explanation of the forces that led me to undertake it and a description of some of the signposts that guided me along the way. This guidance came in various forms. Dreams and visions were given to me. Mysterious strangers passed on messages. Meaningful coincidences were arranged for my edification and instruction. Even miracles were worked on occasion. In this way I was trained for over three years in the skills required to find the stash. Once the training was complete I was shown exactly where to look for it, each item marked with a kind of 'X' to identify it for me. I was even given a key with which to unlock the lid of the treasure chest, supplied exactly when I needed it by a kind of cosmic delivery service.

Of course, the treasure itself is also on display. I call it the September-11 Code, and when you view it you will hopefully realize that it is far more precious than gold or gems or any other material thing. The September-11 Code is a message to you about our current age, and as you read it you will begin to view recent events from the perspective of the encoder. The meaning thereby given them is likely very different from what you currently believe, so be prepared to put your opinions aside and hear what he has to say. I have a feeling you will never forget it, or look at the world around you in the same way again.

The September-11 Code is mostly found within one version of the Christian Bible and one cataclysmic event, witnessed by the entire world. However, its influence has extended to other events appearing on the world stage, products of western culture and even natural phenomena. Buildings were named for architects, plots were given to authors and screenwriters, sentences were constructed for translators, events were timed with split-second accuracy and astronomical alignments were precisely calibrated, all in preparation for the playing out of a horrific, yet enthralling real-life drama at the turn of the millennium.

Given the awesome scope of the phenomenon I am describing and the extraordinary calling I received to investigate it, you may not be surprised to hear me say that it was created by the force or intelligence or being we call 'God'. That's an extraordinary claim, I know, but, since the reality of the code is all-but-indisputable and its authorship far beyond human capability, I think we have no option but to accept that a higher intelligence was the author. Anyway, God has signed his work, so you can be confident of its authenticity. I'm going to assume that God is the author from now on, rather than qualify any statements I make about the origin and purpose of the code.

For those who find that difficult to believe, I don't blame you. God's gifts are placed on our doorstep while we look elsewhere, so it may be tempting to imagine that they arrived by some other means and that the idea of a Heavenly Provider is just a comforting fantasy. But just because we may not have seen him doesn't mean he isn't there. You can't see the atmosphere, but if you have ever watched leaves spiraling round on a windy day, you will have deduced the presence of a swirling vortex of air. Those of us who have received gifts of Spirit have concluded that there is a giver.

Although it's an extraordinary story, I'm not extraordinary in any way. I'm a thinker, certainly, but not a big-time intellectual and I have no real academic credentials. I'm somewhat shy and introspective, a little obsessive (although, for what I had to do, that was a distinct advantage) and generally feel out of place in the world, unless I'm walking or driving in my beloved countryside. I'm working class, if that description still has any meaning, live in a small village and work for a modest salary. Although I'm a Christian, I'm a pretty lame one and I'm no theologian or Bible scholar. Yet it was given to me to find the September-11 Code, so, although I have no idea why I was chosen for such an honor, I did the best I could. I hope I've done it justice.

In case any of you are worrying about it, there isn't any head-spinning mathematics in this book (the message of the code will spin your head right round anyway). There are numbers taken from the Bible and from recent events, a few geometric figures and four substitution schemes by which numbers replace the written word, thereby acting as a bridge to a second, hidden, layer of information. That's right: God uses numerology. He'll use any method he can to get through to us, spinning the humblest threads with consummate skill to form awesome tapestries of meaning before our very eyes.

I've recorded everything as accurately as I can recall it, helped by the many notes I took, usually as soon as possible after the events I describe occurred. I arranged the material in chronological order too, so you can see how I gradually awakened to the nature and enormity of my task and in the hope that you will go through a similar process of revelation and discovery. The treasure on display here is by no means all I've found, but I want you to be dazzled by the magnificence of the code and its message, which a barrow-load of numbers, tables and diagrams would only obscure. Therefore I've kept these to an absolute minimum. It reads better that way and you'll still understand what the code is saying.

The stated dedications include a woman in a shop I returned from before I started this introduction. I once saw an angel in that shop, standing exactly where she stood. But this woman wasn't an angel, just another Christmas shopper. She tried to do me a small kindness by letting me go in front of her. However, the shop assistant had already started ringing up her groceries, so it was too late. She didn't fail, though. By her thoughtfulness she lifted my mood and inspired me to start writing. She seemed to embody the spirit of Christmas, almost obliterated now by the forces of commerce, which have claimed the festival of Christ's birth for their own. So, in addition to my family, I am writing this book for her, the unknown shopper.

Bill Downie
9/24/2011

Chapter 1

An Enlightening Encounter

Do not forget to entertain strangers, for by so doing some people have entertained angels without knowing it.
Hebrews 13.2

One night, when I was a small boy, I had the following dream: *I am being chased along a corridor by an evil and very angry witch. I run as fast as I can to escape her, eventually reaching a door. I grab the handle, turn it, open the door and run through. But there is a second door behind it, and this has an apple for a handle! I frantically grab the apple anyway, open the door and run through that doorway too. On the other side is an abyss, into which I plunge headlong …*

That dream has haunted me all my life, every now and then rising to the surface of my mind for an explanation. But given what I know now, I think I finally understand it. The dream was letting me know about a future event, one that would send shockwaves around the world and so far back in time that it would mysteriously give rise to my dream, almost forty years beforehand. What was the event? It was the attacks on the World Trade Center and the Pentagon, on 11 September, 2001.

The two doors symbolized the twin towers, the World Trade Center and the Pentagon, and even the two cities with which they were associated; the second door with the apple handle was New York, the Big Apple. The witch represented a destructive force bearing down on them. My falling into the abyss represented the fall of the towers. I think the dream was also telling me that I would 'open the door' to an understanding of why the attacks occurred and what they represented. The apple could even have symbolized the fact that I am inputting these words on an Apple computer; dreams often combine several meanings in one symbol.

As well as showing up in one boy's dreams, 9/11 influenced writers, filmmakers, architects, biblical prophets, the course of history and even the movements of the spheres, warping space–time around it like a gravitational singularity. Its staggering message was encoded in detail within the event itself and this message was repeated and expanded upon within one version of the Christian Bible: the New International Version (NIV) 1984 edition.[1] The NIV Bible is the most popular modern English version of the Bible and now outsells all other versions, including the KJV Bible. If a modern version had to be used, the NIV was the best candidate. Later I will describe how I was given the NIV Bible's 1984 edition for decoding (appropriately, it was the 2001 reprint of that edition). I will also relate the story of how I was miraculously given a key that showed me how to unlock the code it contains; I couldn't have cracked the code without that key.

I was given additional help in many other ways, especially through dreams and through images that came to me as I fell asleep or woke up. Some of these dreams and visions I will continue to relate throughout the book. Indeed my calling to this unusual assignment came through an extended vision, which took place three-and-a-half years before 9/11.

One April morning in 1998 I woke up to find myself in the presence of three radiant lights. These were as dazzling as spotlights to me, even though my eyes were still closed. They also had a presence that I found very unsettling. Face to face with them, I suddenly felt very small and exposed (figure 1)

As you can see, the lights were disc-shaped and arranged to suggest a perfect triangle. They were also differentiated by color. The top disc was a pearly white color, whereas the lower discs had a creamy yellow tinge. For about twenty seconds I lay there, refusing to interact with them. Then, plucking up a little courage

Figure 1 The Author's Vision

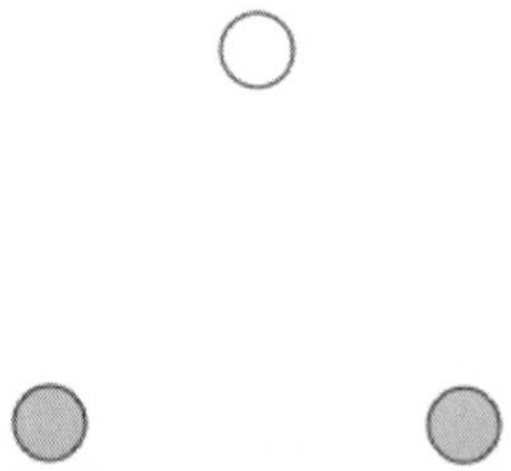

(and though my eyes were still closed), I focused on the yellow disc on the right. For one glorious second I made contact with a heavenly realm, filled with softness and love. But a second was all I got, before all three lights simultaneously winked out.

The experience triggered a dramatic change in me, starting with a new belief in the reality of God. By this I mean that I realized I wasn't really alone in the universe, a skin-encapsulated ego separate from all else, but was connected to something larger. In the past my ideas about God had changed from a simple belief in a Heavenly Father, to rejection of the teachings of my Baptist Sunday school teachers and adoption of the naturalistic worldview offered by science. Lately, however, I had been finding scientific naturalism unbearably drab and restrictive. That April morning a new faith began to blossom in me, like a flower pushing through melting snow. But I wasn't returning to the simple faith of my childhood, which I had long since outgrown. I was going forward to a new, more adult, understanding of God.

The trio of lights were rich in symbolic potential. My first thought was that they stood for the Trinity, with the white disc standing for the Father and the two yellow discs the Son and the Holy Spirit. However, even if that was true there was further significance, because the three parts of the Trinity are supposed to be 'co-equal, co-eternal and consubstantial' and the two-color scheme was suggesting some kind of differentiation. Another possibility was that they represented the Tree of Life, from the

Jewish mystical tradition known as Kabbalah (figure 2).

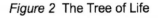

Figure 2 The Tree of Life

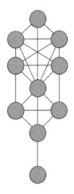

This diagram shows what are regarded as ten 'emanations' of God, properly called *sephiroth*. My vision may have corresponded to the top three sephiroth. These are collectively known as the supernal sephiroth and are thought to be the highest of the emanations, existing on a plane of divine energy. If the white disc in my vision was the topmost sephirah, called *Kether* (crown/divine will), the lower two discs would then be the second and third sephiroth, called *Chockmah* (wisdom) and *Binah* (understanding). Kether is considered neutral, whereas Chockmah is masculine and Binah feminine.

Students of Kabbalah are numerologists and see special significance in numbers, including those found in the Hebrew Bible (the Christian Old Testament). The word 'sephiroth' literally means 'enumerations' or 'counting' and the first three sephiroth are associated with the numbers 1, 2 and 3. The disc I contacted would then be Chockmah, which is masculine and given the number 2. There is an interesting analogy here with Jesus Christ, who is the second person of the Trinity and of course masculine.

The triangular orientation and two-color scheme of the discs in my vision also suggested a series of numbers, known as triangular numbers. My vision corresponded to triangle 3, the second triangular number. The colors showed how the series builds up, so triangle 3 is 1 + 2. Triangle 10, the fourth in the series, is 1 + 2 + 3 + 4 (figure 3).

Figure 3 The First Four Triangular Numbers

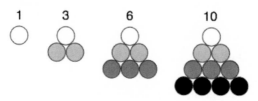

Many other series of 2D figures, such as squares, pentagons, hexagons and stars (hexagrams), can be built from discs. Series of 3D figures, such as cubes, tetrahedrons and pyramids, can be built from spheres.

After my vision I felt an irresistible urge to read as much as I could on religion, spirituality, philosophy, the paranormal and similar topics. I had previously given those sections of bookstores a wide berth, convinced that such topics were for those who needed a crutch to get through life. Now I made a beeline for them every time, choosing a title that took my fancy and devouring it in a few days.

As I read these books I began to change inside. For instance, I began to have vivid, symbolic dreams. In one I was a brown trout swimming in a stream, then leaping out of the water onto land, whereupon I turned into a brightly colored eagle, gorging on raw meat and radiating immense power. In another I was a beetle, marching along in clockwork fashion. A hand reached down and lifted me up, at which point I transformed into a multicolored bird of paradise.

More intriguingly, I began to get flashes of future events, coming in dreams or images. They warned me of significant events ahead, including extreme weather, people to watch out for and births or deaths. These events could be just around the corner or far into the future. An example of my precognitions is the dream with which I began this book. Here is another: *I am looking at a patch of lawn which has been dug up and has flowers planted in it. A voice twice says the word 'stroke'.* Next day my wife's uncle suffered a stroke, the first he had ever had, which proved fatal. The dream was obviously a warning of his death and the burial we would attend.

I realized that I was on some kind of spiritual journey, and as I read and experienced more that journey took me to a magical place, where my inner and outer lives merged into one. On Christmas Eve, 1998, I went to the library and borrowed *The Road Less Travelled*, M. Scott Peck's famous call to psychological wholeness and spiritual growth. I had noticed it in bookstores for years, but initially had no interest in it. Then I would pick it up for a flick-through, promising myself I would read it one day. Then I saw the book in the library on Christmas Eve and knew that the time was right to read it. That's how it works with books like that: you have to be ready to receive their wisdom.

That day I had also taped Frank Capra's *It's A Wonderful Life!*, about George Bailey, the do-gooder who is driven to the brink of suicide by his fellow townsman and nemesis, the avaricious Henry Potter. But Bailey is saved by an angel called Clarence, who jumps into the river while Bailey is thinking of throwing himself in, so that he will save Clarence from drowning. Afterwards Clarence shows Bailey how much more of a grip Potter would have had on the town if he hadn't been born. I watched the film on Christmas night, wondering how I'd managed to miss such a treat before. The final scenes with Clarence took place during a snowstorm on Christmas Eve. Afterwards, I looked outside to see that, at 11:50 p.m. and with snow falling and lying, we had just managed a white Christmas ourselves.

I also read *The Road Less Travelled* over Christmas, finishing it around midday on 28 December. Then I remembered that my wife, Karen, had asked me to buy groceries, so I set off for a local supermarket. As I entered the shop, thinking over topics discussed in the book, I suddenly hit on an appealing metaphor for what is wrong with many people's lives and how they can be changed for the better. If a light bulb blows and we are unaware of how it works, we might try creating our own light by burning things. We might burn our possessions, our furniture or even put our house to the torch, just to keep the light going. Of course we are throwing ever more valuable objects into the flames. But all we really have to do is replace the light bulb, so that the electricity can flow and give us cheap light again.

This is how many of us go through life. When the light goes out of our lives we might look to material success for security and fulfillment. We might seek out amusements and diversions. If we are really down we might turn to alcohol, drugs or crime. But these are all temporary fixes, which usually leave us worse off than beforehand and often lead us to exploit or harm others. For real security and fulfillment, all we have to do is reconnect to God, our divine electricity supply. The more I thought the metaphor through, the more apt it seemed to me.

Just then, as I walked along the aisles, buying my groceries and thinking the metaphor over, the strangest thing happened. A little old man stopped me and gesticulated at the light bulbs displayed where we stood, as if he wanted me to get him a pack. I initially got him a single bulb, but he refused it, pointing again at a pack of four bulbs on the top shelf, which I retrieved for him. Thinking nothing of it, I continued with my shopping. When I went to the checkouts to pay, I saw that there were long queues at every checkout except number four, where the little man stood, so I took my place behind him, putting my things down behind his light bulbs. Suddenly, it struck me how unlikely it was that I should be asked for light bulbs when a light bulb metaphor was on my mind. I wasn't sure if it was anything more than coincidence, though.

At this point I noticed something even odder: the little man, who had a twinkle in his eye I will never forget, was dressed like Clarence in *It's A Wonderful Life!*, the film I had taped four days before and watched for the first time on Christmas day. Spooked, I paid for my shopping and went home. Later I realized that the name of the shop, 'Scotmid', incorporated M. Scott Peck's middle name and first initial. In later correspondence with Dr. Peck, he wrote that he collected light bulb jokes.

On 21 February, 1999, I finished *Further along the Road Less Travelled* (the sequel to *The Road*), exploring the issues of psychological health and spiritual growth in more depth. Afterwards, I made myself a slice of toast. However, in doing that I managed to set the grill on fire. The sound of the smoke alarm wakened my two young daughters, so I went to their room and settled them down. Then I switched off the bedroom light, so we could all see the phosphorescent stars and planets I had stuck to the ceiling. But at this point something strange happened: as I looked up at the ceiling, the bedroom light twice switched itself on and off. These were deliberate flashes, lasting about a second each, not flickers. I recalled the metaphor I had come up with after reading *The Road*, about turning to God for Light instead of burning things to create our own light, and came to the stunned realization that I might have just gotten a reminder of its message. I later tried to copy what I'd seen by wiggling the switch, but the light was either on or off.

With some trepidation I borrowed a third book by M. Scott Peck, *People of the Lie*, finishing it on 6 March, 1999. This is a penetrating study of human evil and how it might be scientifically recognized and overcome. Given the events following my completion of the other two books, I was aware of the possibility of another mysterious communication. I was not to be disappointed. Two light bulbs blew in the house as I was reading the book, so Karen asked me to buy some more. After I'd finished it I went to Scotmid to get them. In addition to the light bulbs I was to get a bottle of wine and a loaf of bread (requested by Karen). I was also going to a local takeaway for fish and chips (requested by my daughters).

Walking through the supermarket, I anxiously waited for something to happen, wondering how this would be possible when I was in a state of acute sensitivity about every action I was taking. I bought the light bulbs, bread and wine then went to the checkout. Then, as I emptied my basket of groceries, I noticed that, along with the light bulbs that connected the experiences, I had bought items with biblical associations: bread and wine. I also realized with a start that I was about to buy a third biblical food: fish. Bread and wine symbolize the body and blood of Christ, and the outline of a fish is an ancient Christian symbol. They are also linked with Jesus' miracles. His first was turning water into wine (John 2.9). Others were the feeding of 5000 people with a few loaves and fishes (Matthew 14, Mark 6, Luke 9, John 6) and the miraculous catch of 153 fish (John 21.11).

As I was leaving the takeaway a man walked in, apparently on cue, and asked for a black pudding (blood sausage), then changed the order to a white pudding (sausage); black to white suggested evil to good. I asked Karen over dinner that evening what she thought were the three items of food or drink most associated with the Bible. 'Bread, wine and fish,' she answered, almost without hesitation.

A month later, Karen and I took an Easter break in St. Andrews in Scotland, during which I read most of *In Search of Stones*, a semi-autobiographical account of a trip Dr. Peck and his wife had made to the UK, where they toured around looking for standing stones. We returned from our own vacation on Easter Monday itself, which was 12 April, 1999. After unpacking, I read a little more of the book. This included a section describing their visit to the famous Callanish stones, situated on the Isle of Lewis, in the Outer Hebrides. The visit was memorable to him because of an incident involving his wife, Lily. As they drove to the stones, Lily announced that she needed to go to the toilet. However, there was no toilet at Callanish and the toilets at the nearby Carloway Broch were shut, this being a Sunday and 'the Sabbath' still being observed fairly scrupulously on that remote island. The Pecks then had to drive fifteen miles before finding a toilet adjoining a small, isolated church.

Easter Monday was also my father's birthday, so in the evening we visited my parents to drop off a present for him. My parents had also gone for an Easter break, in their case to the northwest of Scotland (although we had no idea precisely where they'd gone) and had returned on Easter Monday like us. As we walked in the door I asked my parents about their own vacation. To my utter astonishment they told us the following story. They had visited the Callanish stones the day before, which was Easter Sunday. While they were there my mother had needed to go to the toilet, but the facilities were locked so they had to drive fifteen miles before they found a toilet adjoining a small, remote church. *This sequence of events was exactly the same as in the passage I had just read about the experience of the Pecks.* My parents were also about the same age as the Pecks and had even stayed at the same hotel.

The correspondences between the experiences of the Pecks and my parents constituted the fourth and final message I was given: just as Lily Peck and my mother found 'relief' at a church, so we can find relief from life's difficulties by turning to God. In fact, that's essentially what all four messages were saying to me, and this unifying theme persuaded me they were real signs from above and not meaningless coincidences. This was something I needed to hear at that time, because my life was filled with conflict, both external and internal, and I felt a lot like George Bailey did before Clarence came to rescue him. But even as I stood in awe and gratitude before a God who was offering himself as my helper and guide, I marveled that he would go to such extraordinary lengths to arrange these events just for my private benefit.

I sensed how unusual my experiences were so I recorded every detail. As I did so, I couldn't help noticing that the number four seemed to be an integral part of them. I was given four messages in a little over four months (these precisely covering the period from Christmas to Easter), ending in April, the fourth month, and involving four books by M. Scott Peck. The first message was given to me on the fourth-last day of the year and the little man had insisted on four light bulbs and stood at checkout four. The fourth message was also particularly marked with this number: four people were involved (my parents and the Pecks), and it took place four months, less four days, short of my fortieth birthday. The number four had to be important in some way.

I began to gather information on the number four and eventually came across the writings of E. W. Bullinger, an English biblical scholar and Anglican who lived in the 19th century. His classic work *Number in Scripture*, published on the internet, is a detailed examination of biblical numbers and their spiritual meanings.[2] According to Bullinger, four is linked with God's creations and so it is the number representing *the world*. For this it is perfectly suited, as for example there are four seasons, four points of the compass and four divisions of the day.

Because of the timings of the encounters I'd had, it occurred to me to count the number of days between them and also to marker dates such as the end of the millennium. When I did that I made a shocking, thrilling discovery. The subject of the third book I had read, *People of the Lie*, was human evil. Was it just an accident, then, that I finished it on 6 March, 1999, which was 666 days before the end of the second millennium? I had a feeling it wasn't. 666 is of course the number of 'the beast', an appellation used in the Bible's final, apocalyptic book. The beast is a creature or creatures appearing on the world stage during the end times, empowered by Satan, the fallen angel who opposes God's plans and actively seeks our destruction. The number 666 and the fact that it related Peck's book on human evil to the end of the millennium, an 'end times' marker date for many Christians, put a prophetic coloring on what I was beginning to see was a mysterious, multilayered communication, concerned with far more than one man's private troubles.

Around this time I had another dream which affected me deeply: *I am standing in a building watching the approach of a devastating whirlwind. A woman is calling my name, over and over. If the whirlwind strikes I may not survive, so I fervently hope it misses. But it heads straight for the building I am in and engulfs me. Another voice speaks, saying 'Hurricane Vincent'.* The name Vincent means 'victorious' and comes from the Latin root word *vincere*, meaning 'to conquer'. In Christian tradition the wind is associated with the Holy Spirit, which 'blows where it will', influencing lives and events for its own purposes. I sensed the approach of that overwhelming force in my own life and wondered what was to become of me.

Chapter 2

Crows and Other Messengers

If you wish to upset the law that all crows are black, you mustn't seek to show that no crows are; it is enough if you prove one single crow to be white.
    William James

The message I had been given seemed in essence to be that I had to let God into my life, that without his guidance I would be lost and that I had to actively seek that guidance, presumably through prayer and church attendance (my parents' experience suggested I would find 'relief' in a church). But that's not easy for me: I'm very independent and generally hate asking for help. I certainly felt lost, though. After half a lifetime filled with conflict I had a lot of painful memories that I just couldn't get past and continually fretted over. Having recently been promoted at work, I was also going through a baptism of fire as a manager. I was trying to handle three difficult colleagues at once and they seemed to be highlighting every weakness I had, both as a manager and as a person.

The low point of this affair came early in 1999. I was overwhelmed with staff problems and was handling it so badly (mainly because my judgment was clouded by rage) that I was almost daily making the situation worse. One day, when a plan to bring a new member of staff into the department to ease my troubles backfired on me, I suddenly realized that I'd reached the end of my tether. An awful feeling of hopelessness began to well up inside me. Simultaneously, however, I began to feel very calm. I felt myself relax more and more until, as best as I can describe it, my mind seemed to expand well beyond the boundaries of my skull, something I would have thought impossible. I also began to sense the presence around me of something very holy. As I became more attuned to the 'field of consciousness' that enveloped me, I detected separate areas of awareness, radiating a poignant sense of the sacredness of life and reminding me not to waste my own. I knew then that I was somehow part of them and that they were always around me, gently guiding me.

The experience lasted for about twenty minutes then gently faded. For the next few hours I felt what I can best describe as an inner stillness, bearing the same relationship to my usual mental state as a clear pond has to a whirlpool. My awareness had regained a subtlety of feeling normally drowned under a barrage of mostly negative emotions and for a few precious hours I was reconnected with my inner self, with all of life and with the Source of all things.

Over the previous few weeks I had been repeatedly having variations of a dream, involving crossing a body of water. The following dream was typical: *I am standing on the shore of a bay. The water is choppy and filled with sharks and other dangerous creatures. The entrance to the bay is a narrow channel, beyond which is the open sea. Beyond that is a beautiful, crystalline city, sparkling in the sun. I know I have to get to that city but I am afraid to cross the water.* The city is a metaphor for heaven and the choppy, forbidding water is the sin that separates me from it. The narrow channel through which I have to pass suggests the birth canal and thus the Christian concept of being 'born again'. A year or so later, reading *The Archetypes and the Collective Unconscious*, by psychologist and mystic Carl Jung, I came upon his account of a dream had by a 19th-century theologian. He was standing at the top of a hill looking down at a deep, fast-flowing river. A path ran from where he stood straight into the river, then continued up the far slope to a castle that stood on the other side of the valley. This was identical to my own dream in all the essentials. Jung's interpretation was that the castle represented the Self, or God-image, and the river represented the unconscious mind, the contents of which the theologian would have to face if he was to grow. I marveled that two people unknown to each other could have such strikingly similar dreams a hundred years apart and realized that there may be something in Jung's notion of a collective unconscious, where archetypal forces influence the patterns of our individual lives. The long-gone theologian had refused this invitation to psycho-spiritual growth, which I could understand, as I did not want to face my own demons either. But I also suspected – and my reading material of late insisted – that this was the only way forward.

The crisis at work continued. One day in March 1999 I was told I was to lose my position as laboratory manager, largely because of accusations one staff member was making against me, accusations I knew to be largely untrue. Distraught, I went for a walk next day to try to get my head together, choosing a route that took me alongside a local canal for part of the way. As I walked along the canal bank, deep in thought about my situation at work, my attention was grabbed by a nearby crow, which chattered noisily, as if to get my attention, then flew towards me over the vegetation growing along the bank. It passed in front of me, almost brushing me with its wings, then swung round and veered back along the same path. However, this time instead of passing me it dropped into the water directly in front of me, then slowly and awkwardly swam in a straight line across the water until it reached the far bank. Then it climbed up onto the bank, looked round at me and flew away.

I watched this spectacle with open-mouthed astonishment. The crow certainly wasn't washing itself. Why, then, would it swim across the entire width of the canal directly in front of me? Then it came to me: the crow was enacting the water-crossing dreams I'd been having! This jaw-dropping display shocked me into accepting that the awakening I was undergoing was very real and also seemed to be encouraging me over my crisis at work: *you are in a difficult situation, but if you fight on you will get through it.* Heartened by the incident, I wrote a report on my situation at work that saved the day for me. After some staff changes my problems eased and I breathed a sigh of relief, suspecting I'd been through some kind of rite of passage and knowing I couldn't have made it without the help of that aquatic crow. Later, I learned that in some cultures crows are believed to be spiritual messengers.

This experience, like some of the others, could partly be explained by synchronicity, Jung's word for the meaningful coincidences that seem to happen at times of psycho-spiritual crisis, outer events mirroring inner changes. Synchronicity would explain why the actions of the crow reflected my dream life at that time. But, although I knew that they were highly intelligent, my experience of crows and rooks was that they rarely if ever swam and they avoided contact with humans, so it seemed to me that there had to be something even stranger at work here. The animal had temporarily been possessed by a force: one which was prepared to go to great lengths to gain my attention, and which had a seemingly infinite number of methods at its disposal for doing so.

On 5 July, 1999, I went to Scotmid to pick up a few groceries. I've forgotten what I bought that day but I do remember a very strange incident that happened there. I was followed into the shop by a very pretty girl of about eighteen, who skipped along the aisle I was in and cooed as she passed me to get my attention. She had a kind of glow about her that really made her stand out in that small-town supermarket on a Monday evening and I had the feeling that she was not the shop's usual kind of customer. Seeing, as I walked up to the checkout, that she was at the back of the queue, and not really feeling up to receiving another mysterious message, I hung back to allow other shoppers to get between us. But somehow she maneuvered herself into being right in front of me again. After the girl was served she turned round and gave me a long and embarrassing stare, before skipping out the door.

This was the second mysterious stranger I'd met in Scotmid and I noticed that there were parallels between the encounters. For a start, the encounters began in the middle of the supermarket and ended at the checkout. Then there were the dates of these encounters: 12/28/1998 and 7/5/1999. The digits in both dates added to forty: $1 + 2 + 2 + 8 + 1 + 9 + 9 + 8 = 40$, and $7 + 5 + 1 + 9 + 9 + 9 = 40$. I checked my own birth date: 8/8/1959. Those digits summed to forty as well. 9/11 still hadn't occurred at this point, but I later noticed that I had been 14,576, or 911 x 4 x 4, days old on this date. As a lone statistic this would mean very little, but I was to discover that neither the dates of these encounters nor the date on which I'd been born were accidents.

Forty is regarded as a watershed age in many cultures. Around this age, people often start to engage less with the outside world and more with their inner life, often beginning a spiritual search. For instance, traditionally, a man may not study Kabbalah unless he is married with three children and in his fortieth year. In the Bible, forty is the number of trials, testing and temptation: Jesus lived in the wilderness for forty days and was tempted by Satan; the Israelites wandered in the wilderness of Egypt for forty years. Having gone through a trial of my own in my fortieth year and survived it, I suspected that my own forty years of 'wandering in the desert' (which fairly accurately described my life up to that point) were coming to an end.

The experiences continued unabated. On 28 December, 1999, I took my two daughters to a local shopping center, because they wanted to spend some of their Christmas money. Thinking of how much *The Road Less Travelled* had meant to me, I decided to buy it, so I walked to the cash dispenser to draw out some money. As I made my way there a woman walked up to me, whistled four notes into my face and walked away. At the same time a song had been playing in my head, called 'Better Off

Alone', by Alice Deejay,[3] and the four notes she had whistled were the ones running through my head at that time. She even whistled them at the same pitch (I was an amateur musician for many years and have a fairly good musical ear). The song's only lyrics were 'Do you think you're better off alone?' and 'Talk to me'.

I drew out some cash and went to a bookshop to buy *The Road*. Although the book meant a lot to me, I felt a pang of guilt spending money on myself so soon after Christmas. There was a half-price sale on in the shop but *The Road* wasn't a sale item, so I was going to have to pay the full price of £6. However, when I got to the checkout, the woman serving (whom I'd never seen before) charged me only £1, saying, 'See, you've got peace of mind already!', as if she knew I had been feeling guilty. Too dumbfounded to answer, I just took the book and went home with my daughters.

At home, checking my diary, I saw that my encounters with the two women had happened exactly one year to the day and hour since my initial encounter with the little man, which was perhaps also why I'd been charged £1. If the two experiences really were related, then the lyrics of the chart hit I'd been listening to – 'Do you think you're better off alone?' and 'Talk to me' – must have been a reminder of the messages I'd received a year earlier, about connecting to God. There was even a link to the number four, through the four notes whistled at me. Come to think of it that made four enigmatic strangers I'd encountered, all in shops and shopping centers.

I wondered who these people were and how they could be capable of creating such powerful and deeply symbolic, yet subtle and highly personal experiences. Every encounter was pregnant with meaning and perfectly choreographed, with me as an unwitting, bewildered participant. In dressing like Clarence the angel in *It's A Wonderful Life!*, could the little man have been revealing their identity to me? Did I always meet these people in shops because angels are God's messengers and you go shopping to get messages (I'm a Scot and 'messages' is a Scottish term for groceries)? It was a thrilling possibility, but also a terrifying one, as I wasn't at all sure that I was up to realizing whatever plans they had for me.

* * *

The millennium came and went without the Y2K bug or any other signs of Armageddon. In fact, as I stood outside at midnight on 31 December, enjoying the fireworks dancing over nearby Edinburgh, I saw it as a metaphor for the dawning of a new light in the world. I wondered how many people were aware, though, that 1 January, 2000 was not the beginning of the third millennium: that fell on 1 January, 2001. By all accounts it didn't matter at all to most people, but to me, absorbed in esoteric calculations like some medieval kabbalist, the details of the change from the second to the third millennium were of more than passing concern.

Browsing in a bookstore one day in January 2000, I picked up a book called *More Hot Chocolate for the Mystical Soul,* a compilation of inspiring stories of people's spiritual experiences. One was by a man called Nick Bunick, who claimed that angels communicated to him using the number 444. That stunned me, since I was already three-quarters convinced that angels were using the number four to communicate with me. The story mentioned a book written about him called *The Messengers,* which I eventually tracked down.

I read the book over four days. It was a fascinating story, concerning synchronicities Bunick experienced involving the number 444, communications he received from angels and his apparent connection to the apostle Paul. Even more interesting, though, was the fact that on all four days I, too, had '444' experiences. These climaxed on the final day. I woke up at 4:44 a.m.

While dozing that afternoon I dreamed that a shining, silver Rolls Royce with the registration plate '44' parked at my house. When I woke up my wife Karen phoned to ask me to buy something for her, so I went to the hardware store to get it. I arrived there at 4:44 p.m. As I walked up to the desk the service manager, who was counting cash, said to his assistant, '£44.40'. That evening Karen asked me to get some groceries, so I went to Scotmid again. I bought the items she had asked for and went to the checkout. I was charged £4:44.

My life was taking on a surreal quality, like a waking dream. Outer events reflected my inner journey with uncanny regularity and I began to feel less the center of my own little world and more a player in an unfolding cosmic drama. For example, one day around this period I was driving my car to work, listening to the radio, when suddenly my hand moved of its own accord and changed the station. At that very moment I heard Terry Wogan say 'Just call me an angel'. Another day my lab assistant brought in her feather angel wings to show us. She put them on at 4:44 p.m., unaware that she had done so until I told her. Other people had strange dreams they shared with me. A woman who worked in another department of the company, who knew nothing of my experiences, had the following dream: *I see Bill and everyone else surrounded by angels. Nobody is aware of it except Bill. There are two versions of him and I run back and forth between them.* I didn't understand the doubling in the dream at the time but later on it made deep sense, as you will see.

By this time I knew that the message delivered to me incorporated numerical patterns and I was convinced that I was being invited to investigate them. That suited me, because I'm good with numbers and have the patience to pick away at problems, which helped me win a puzzle-solving competition when I was twenty. So I continued to work on the unusual problem I appeared to have been set, even as I explored the new vistas that were opening up before me.

In *Number in Scripture*, Bullinger stated something about the number four that really got my attention. This was the city number, based on an intriguing fact: in biblical Hebrew letters doubled as numbers, and the letters of the Hebrew word for Damascus, *Dammeseq*, had numerical values that summed to 444. The Hebrew letters in Dammeseq are Daleth, Mem, Shin and Koph, with values 4, 40, 300 and 100. These numbers sum to 444, so this is the numerical value of Dammeseq.[4] Damascus has two distinctions: it is thought to be the oldest city in the world and it was the city that Saul of Tarsus was traveling towards when he famously had a vision that led to his conversion to belief in Jesus Christ. After this he became the apostle Paul, the founder of Christianity.

Was there some personal meaning for me in that number? Was I on my own 'road to Damascus'? Interestingly, the triple four implied three. In the Bible, three represents divine perfection and four represents creation. These sum to seven, the number of spiritual perfection, and multiply to give twelve, the number associated with perfect government under God's rule. So 444 perhaps also implied the idea of creation being brought under God's rule, just as Paul, previously a persecutor of Christians, became an apostle of Christ.

I read more about Christianity, which now began to interest me a little. I also turned my attention to the novel idea that letters could substitute for numbers. I knew about Roman numerals, of course, but it had never occurred to me that letters might double for numbers in other languages and that words themselves could be assigned a numerical value. Still less did I imagine that numbers could have any meaning, beyond the quantity they represented. These ideas, I was to discover, were common currency in many circles, particularly among students of Kabbalah, the Jewish mystical school from which the Tree of Life originated. In Kabbalah, words and phrases with identical or related numerical values are said to be 'explanatory of each other': they are also related through meaning. The practice of calculating and interpreting the numerical values of words (and phrases) is generally known as *gematria*.

One night I was told during a numinous dream that I was to 'work' with a woman, who I was shown so that I would recognize her. I didn't know her at the time but a couple of months later she came to work in my department. It turned out that she was interested in spirituality, so I gave her *The Messengers* to read. Soon after this she told me that she had discovered an internet forum where people discussed the numerical values of English words and suggested I look into it, which I did.

The simplest and most natural way of giving the letters of the English alphabet a number value is to swap a letter with its place value in the alphabet. So A =1, B = 2, C = 3, etc, down to Z = 26. These are called *ordinal values* (table 2.1)

Table 2.1 The Ordinal Value System		
A = 1	J = 10	S = 19
B = 2	K = 11	T = 20
C = 3	L = 12	U = 21
D = 4	M = 13	V = 22
E = 5	N = 14	W = 23
F = 6	O = 15	X = 24
G = 7	P = 16	Y = 25
H = 8	Q = 17	Z = 26
I = 9	R = 18	

If we sum the number values of the letters in any English word, or by extension, phrase, we can give it a numerical value, as shown here (the 'o' in brackets means 'ordinal value'):

God (o) = 7 + 15 + 4 = 26

At first I just played around with numbering words, working out the values of words related to anything spiritual. Here are a few of my results.

Lord (o) = 49

God (o) = 26

Jesus (o) = 74
Christ (o) = 77
Holy (o) = 60
Spirit (o) = 91

That meant the phrases 'Jesus Christ' and 'Holy Spirit' had the same ordinal value.

Jesus Christ (o) = 151
Holy Spirit (o) = 151

Later, I found that the number 151 was a kind of 'strange attractor' for phrases relating to Jesus Christ, phrases which were 'explanatory of each other' in kabbalistic parlance:

Jesus is Lord (o) = 151
Christ the King (o) = 151
Lord of Hosts (o) = 151
The Sacrificial Lamb (o) = 151
The Incarnation (o) = 151

Was anything going on here? Modern English has a huge vocabulary and therefore there would be many phrases unrelated to Jesus Christ with numerical value 151. Conversely, though, it was uncanny how this number was attached to many of the names and titles we had happened to give him. Perhaps even in modern English, words and phrases conveying a particular meaning (or at least a small subset of emotionally charged words and phrases) tend to crystallize around certain numbers. The reasons why the number 151 may have been the 'attractor' for the above phrases will become obvious in later chapters.

Another interesting phenomenon I stumbled upon was the fact that the words 'Lord' and 'God' are closely linked to the numbers seven and thirteen:

Lord (o) = 49 = 7 x 7

God (o) = 26 = 13 + 13

I already knew that seven and thirteen have a geometric relationship. In chapter 1 I showed how triangular numbers can be represented as triangles composed of evenly spaced discs. In studying triangular numbers I learned that every third such triangle can merge with an inverted copy of itself to give a star (hexagram). The first figure that can create a star is triangle 10 (figure 4).

Figure 4 Triangle 10 merging with itself
to give star 13/hexagon 7

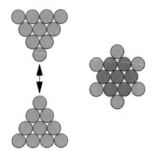

Some of the discs in the star are common to both triangles. When these are highlighted an internal hexagon is shown, and the entire figure becomes the Star of David. Since the Star of David is the modern symbol of Judaism and an ancient symbol of Christ, it appeared to be serendipitous that a link should exist between this figure and the two most important English words for the Judeo-Christian God.

I later discovered that words and phrases related to spiritual things often have either 7 or 13 as a factor. For instance 'Christ' (77), 'divine' (63) and 'Light' (56) share 7 as a factor; 'angel' (39), 'Devil' (52), 'Risen' (65) and 'God the Father' (117) are multiples of 13. Even more interesting was the fact that 'Spirit' and 'the Father' sum to 91, which is 7 x 13 and a triangular number.

Furthermore, the shape of a triangle represents the Christian concept of the Trinity. These improbable connections suggested to me that some kind of force might be guiding the development of the English language to create numerical and geometric relationships between words and phrases with similar meanings, for me a novel and exciting idea. I still wasn't totally convinced though.

Around this time I had another powerful dream, which gave the impression of being the 'dream of my life': *I am Mr. Spock and I descend to Earth from an orbiting artificial moon, on an important but difficult and even dangerous mission. I have something to tell people, something which is very important but which I know they will not want to hear. When I do tell people they start crying and screaming, even assaulting me.* This epic dream suggested to me the general nature of what I was to do, although the details were still a mystery.

I began to read the Bible, which I found tough going (especially since I only had the King James Version [KJV], written in archaic English) but which I was beginning to appreciate, in the light of what little spiritual understanding I had recently gained. One night, as I was reading my Bible in bed, my bedside lamp flashed off and on, as if someone had flicked the switch. It was exactly the same experience as the one I had had in my daughters' bedroom over a year beforehand. The verse I was reading was Matthew 7.21: 'Not everyone that saith unto me, Lord, Lord, shall enter into the kingdom of heaven; but he that doeth the will of my Father which is in heaven' (KJV). If I was to become a Christian, it wasn't merely to sit around praising Jesus.

In October 2000 I finally decided I would go to church. I chose the local parish church and set off with my old Sunday school Bible in my pocket. As I approached the church I felt like I was walking through treacle, so nervous was I, but I went in anyway and quite enjoyed the service. Next day at work I had another odd experience (although by now I was getting quite used to them). While relaxing after lunch I almost fell asleep, at which I distinctly heard a male voice say 'Finally friends'. This was obviously a comment on my first visit to church since I was dragged there as a boy and it seemed like an encouragement. I had heard of the 'still, small voice' of the Holy Spirit and this was one of the first times I'd heard it myself – if that's what it was.

After that I began to get into the habit of praying then taking little catnaps, because that was when I usually had these experiences. The trick was to get close to falling asleep without actually dropping off, entering the twilight zone between wakefulness and sleep where these experiences most often happened. If the 'seeing' was good I would quickly get a succession of pictures or short movie clips, hear voices, see words or experience some combination of these phenomena. They always contained useful information and seemed to have been designed to lead me along the spiritual path, one step at a time.

I continued going to church as well. I was made very welcome there and was soon invited to take The Alpha Course,[5] a well-known introductory course in the Christian faith. The course was enjoyable and my fellow Alpha students were friendly, thoughtful and enquiring, all of which dispelled some of the preconceptions I had about a faith that has a very bad press these days. Sometimes I thought it deserved that bad press, but other times it seemed to me as if secularists were simply out to bring down the Church. Now I had a chance to find out what it was really like and I was pleasantly surprised. Christianity was more fun on the inside than it looked from without.

I continued to read voraciously, particularly seeking out spiritual titles, including those by M. Scott Peck, who had become a Christian soon after penning *The Road*. One summer evening I lay in bed reading his most devotional work, *What Return Can I Make?*, a series of essays on the Christian journey (coauthored with Marilyn von Waldner and Patricia Kay). In one of them he stated his opinion that God was a purely creative force and therefore incapable of destroying anything. As I considered this theological position an inner voice countered Peck's words with the forceful statement "God *can* destroy!" Feeling a shiver of foreboding, I put down the book and drifted off to sleep.

Chapter 3

The Key to the Code

Comfort the afflicted and afflict the comfortable.
Finley Peter Dunne

On the morning of 11 September, 2001, I woke up to hear a male voice speak the following words: 'Serpent power'. I wrote them down and went off to work. In Genesis 3, Satan, in the guise of a serpent, persuaded Eve to take a fruit from the tree of knowledge of good and evil, expressly against God's wishes. But on the other hand in Exodus 7 God turns Aaron's staff into a snake, which swallows the snakes of his magician adversaries; that particular serpent was doing God's will. I also knew that, according to Hindus, serpent power was the energy involved in a Kundalini awakening, a dramatic, though potentially dangerous, moment of enlightenment. This energy, which, according to Hindus, is normally stored in the 'root chakra' at the base of the spine and is symbolized by a coiled serpent, was also harnessed by men going into battle. So I wasn't sure what was meant by the words I'd heard.

At lunchtime I got into a discussion with some work colleagues about the greed and materialism of western democ-racies: about unfair trading practices and ill-advised bank loans turning many third-world countries into virtual slave states; about the USA in particular running rampant over the world, taking the resources of weaker nations, while leaving behind viral aspects of its way of life such as junk food, theme parks and shopping malls. I finished by stating that in the USA politics, finance, the media and the 'military-industrial complex' were so institutionally corrupt and self-serving that some observers believed that only a revolution of some kind would change the system now. A junior colleague was flying a paper airplane around the room as we spoke.

I left work early that afternoon and drove home, unaware of the apocalyptic events unfolding across the Atlantic Ocean. Around 3 p.m., Karen phoned to tell me that something extraordinary was happening in New York and that I should put the TV on, so I did just that. Then I sat in front of it for eight hours, watching with horror, fascination and an odd sense of unreality as the serpent struck the USA, causing the deaths of 3000 people, the destruction of the twin symbols of global capitalism, and the 'Kundalini awakening' of our sleeping world.

As I absorbed all the news reports, my sense of the unreality of it all was compounded by something else: a growing string of coincidences involving the number eleven. For instance, the date was the 11th, the twin towers resembled a huge eleven, the first airplane to strike was Flight 11 and there were 110 storeys in each tower. In the weeks, months and years that followed, I came across many more of them. For instance: on 19 December, 2001, New York City officials declared that all fires at the site had finally been extinguished, which was 99 (11 x 9) days after 9/11; the sums of the impact times (8:46 a.m. and 9:03 a.m.) was 1749 (11 x 159); the total death toll at the World Trade Center was 2871 (11 x 9 x 29).[6]

The statistics I gathered included curious facts that seemed to indicate that both the World Trade Center and the Pentagon were historically linked with both eleven and 9/11. For instance: New York was the 11th state to join the federal union; Manhattan Island, on which the towers stood, was first seen by Henry Hudson on 11 September, 1609, as he explored the river named after him; work began on the construction of the Pentagon on 11 September, 1941. Bizarrely, the coincidences even extended to people caught up in 9/11. The TV news reporter on the channel I watched was Mark Cviic and the most famous victim was the co-creator of the TV comedy *Frazier*, David Angell.

Could these elevens (and there are many more than I've shown) be accounted for purely by chance? Certainly some of them could. But others, such as the historical events relating the date to the locations and the doubled letters in the names of people caught up in it, were harder to explain away. I sensed from the start that a more likely explanation was synchronicity, which had played such a big part in my life of late. The elevens shone out like a beacon, signaling to those with 'ears to hear' that 9/11 had something important to say to us. According to Bullinger, eleven stands for disorganization, disorder, disintegration and imperfection.[7] I started thinking about the number 11, its biblical meaning and why a cluster of elevens should have gathered around one particular event, unaware that the unseen forces that were guiding my steps had been preparing me for over three years to find the answer to that very question.

* * *

My spiritual experiences continued to increase in frequency and intensity, and I was assailed night and day by a barrage of dreams, visions and signs. One night in October 2001 I had an incredibly vivid dream: *I am falling out of the Light, having just met with God himself. All I remember is being told I had accomplished my life's mission. I float down through the air, looking down on an enormous city at twilight. At the center of this vast metropolis is a humongous tower, perhaps a mile high. I can see the fading sunlight reflecting off its thousands of windows. I continue floating downwards then pass through a roof into a bedroom, landing on the bed. Two dogs, one either side of me, jump at me and I realize they are going to bite my testicles.* This shocked me awake, at which point I heard a voice say, 'It will all be different now.' I looked at the clock: it read 1:11 a.m. For the next two days I felt like a deep-sea diver, walking along the sea floor. I belonged up there with the Light, not down here in the spiritual underworld.

On 10 November, 2001 I went to the Alpha Course's Holy Spirit Weekend, a two-day retreat, during which participants are given a chance to experience the Holy Spirit. On the second day, 11 November, 2001, after the usual lecture tape and group discussions, we had an extended prayer session during which we asked to be filled with the Holy Spirit. Most people said they did experience something and several broke down in tears, but, perhaps because I was tense with expectation, I felt nothing happen to me. Disappointed, I went home.

I was feeling energetic, however, so I decided to clean out the garage. After that I was still full of beans, so I finished wallpapering the bathroom, something I had been dragging my heels over for weeks. By now I felt as if I wanted to run out and talk to people: anybody, even strangers. Why was I wasting time cooped up in the house when I could be out there, getting to know everyone? Suddenly, I realized what was happening. The prayer session had worked after all: this was the Holy Spirit flowing through me, bringing me to myself for the first time in years. I was as different from my usual introspective, world-weary self as day is from night and I was filled with energy, overflowing with joy. I noted that this had happened on the 11th day of the 11th month; I could sense something momentous building.

Next evening I went to the Alpha meeting still filled with Spirit. In previous discussions, several of the participants had shared personal problems with the group and we had listened without judgment and prayed for them. This time I felt moved to share a problem of my own. I admitted to the group that I had long harbored very negative and often violent feelings about an old supervisor, with whom I had locked horns for seven years. The memories of these old conflicts had eaten away at me for over a decade and in fact were slowly killing me. Just admitting this fact seemed to free me somewhat, as it had been a very big deal for me, but I had kept to myself the extent of my hatred for this man. The morning after that, which was 13 November, 2001, I woke up and immediately knew that I was free of all my bitterness towards him, a state that has remained to this day. It was as miraculous as if a cancerous tumor had suddenly disappeared, which in a way was what had happened.

That day, on impulse, I worked out the ordinal values for names and places related to 9/11. The first value I worked out was that of 'Osama bin Laden'.

Osama bin Laden (o) = 110

That seemed too much to be coincidence. I tried 'New York'.

New York (o) = 111

A thrill went through me and I knew with complete certainty that I had found my calling. I spent most of the rest of that day working out number values for words and phrases related to 9/11. Here are a few more of them, beginning with a version of bin Laden's name that he reportedly started using to sign documents after the 9/11 attacks.

Osama bin Muhammad bin Laden (o) = 209 = 11 x 19

The spelling I used for both versions of bin Laden's name was only one of several alternative English spellings of the original Arabic, but it was at least fifty times more popular than any alternative spellings on Google searches, so I felt I was on safe ground using it.

The Pentagon is situated in the county of Arlington, across the Potomac River from Washington DC.

Arlington (o) = 110

Even the date on which the attacks took place was a multiple of eleven.

> September the eleventh, two thousand and one (o) = 440 = 11 x 40

The full names of the four flights that were hijacked summed to another interesting number.

> American Airlines Flight 11 + United Airlines Flight 175 + American Airlines Flight 77 + United Airlines Flight 93 (o) = 911

Good Lord, could that really be coincidence? These highly unlikely numerical correspondences, where none should be, suggested that the numerical synchronicities I had been noticing in my own life were also surrounding 9/11. Suddenly I began to see my own spiritual experiences within a global context. Were the world and I both at a point of transition? My head was reeling with the enormity of it all.

Other interesting numbers turned up too. For instance, the flight numbers of the three airplanes that hit their targets summed to 263, which was also the value of the fullest version of bin Laden's name in English: Osama bin Muhammad bin Awad bin Laden. So I felt that this number also had to be important. Other numbers I found were simply baffling. Nor could I get the values of any of the buildings struck on 9/11 to sum to a multiple of eleven. I recorded them anyway. It was early days and I had found enough to convince me that this was worth a lot more effort.

Two days after that, on 15 November, 2001, I switched on the radio while I was driving to work to hear the opening chords of the overture to Verdi's opera *La Forza del Destino* (*The Force of Destiny*). I love this piece so I listened to it all. That evening, as I was driving home from work, I switched on the radio a second time that day, to again hear the opening chords of *La Forza del Destino*. As I enjoyed the music a second time, I remembered its title and knew that Destiny was now calling me.

That same day my Alpha Course director was reading a passage in her Bible when an inner voice spoke to her: 'This is for Bill.' Startled, she read the passage a second time, whereupon the voice spoke to her again: 'This is for Bill.' Feeling a little shocked, she put her Bible down and made a cup of tea, leaving a plain piece of paper in her Bible as a bookmark. When she reopened her Bible she was astonished to see the very words she had been reading, 1 Thessalonians 5.23–24, printed in large type on the bookmark. What was more, they were addressed 'Dear Bill' and signed 'Love Paul'. Eleven days later she told me what had happened to her, stated she was convinced I was the person to whom the message was addressed and handed me the bookmark. The words printed on the bookmark, which I still have, are reproduced below exactly as they appear on it.

Dear Bill

May God himself, the God of peace, sanctify you through and through. May your whole spirit, soul and body be kept blameless at the coming of our Lord Jesus Christ.
The one who calls you is faithful and he will do it.

Love Paul

I saw the unusual shape made by the body of text: it actually resembled a *key*. Was that what these words were, some kind of key? I noted that the date she received the passage and the date she gave it to me were the 319th and 330th day of 2001 (and the third millennium). Each number was a multiple of eleven.

The version of the Bible my Alpha Course director had been

reading was the New International Version (NIV). A few days later I was handed an NIV New Testament by my oldest daughter, given to me as I was reading a list of my findings so far on the way eleven appeared to be woven into the numerics of 9/11. A week or so after that, Karen went to a bookshop to buy me an NIV Bible for Christmas; I had asked for that version months before, simply because I liked the way it read. As she stood before the Bibles they had for sale, unable to remember which one of the many versions in front of her I had asked for, an NIV Bible fell from the bookshelf into her hands.

If the words on the bookmark really were the key to some type of numerical code, then that code had to be within the NIV Bible. Both the New Testament and the full Bible I had been given were the 1984 editions, so it was probably that edition too. It surely also had something to do with 9/11.

1 Thessalonians was the first letter written by the apostle Paul and is the oldest book in the New Testament. This was the second time the figure of Paul had loomed behind my experiences; the first time was a couple of years beforehand when I read *The Messengers*, the book about Paul that featured the number 444, and which triggered 444 experiences in my own life. I had learned afterwards that 444 was the value of the Hebrew word for Damascus, the city Paul had been traveling towards when a blinding vision converted him from Orthodox Jew to founder of Christianity. Was it possible that this message came from him?

By now I felt as if every day was somehow predestined, the mere acting out of a script already written. I continually worried about fouling up in some way, but also realized that my own personal weaknesses and insecurities were probably being taken into account. Why me, though? Although I considered myself to be a theist at this point, I was anything but religious, hadn't yet become a Christian and hardly knew one end of the Bible from the other. If there was a code in the NIV Bible, or any other version, then surely there were a couple of billion Christians who were better qualified to find it. Later, however, I came to see that my lack of Christian training could be an advantage, because I had no indoctrination to overcome and no particular theological position to defend – and because sometimes a beginner can see what an expert will miss.

The woman who led me to gematria had begun attending a Christian Spiritualist church and was given a mysterious instruction there: 'Remember the blue triangle.' I naturally assumed that the message was for her, but a few days later, after receiving a sign involving a blue triangle and the number 444, I realized that I might have been the intended recipient. I didn't understand what the instruction meant at the time, but kept it at the back of my mind as I continued to gather information. Then, on 18 November, 2001, right at the peak of my mystical experiences, I made my first tentative connection between 9/11 and the Bible. I was looking at the number 216, which is the sum of these words:

Nine eleven + New York (o) = 216
September 11 + New York (o) = 216

As I sat there looking at the number I realized with a start that it is 6 x 6 x 6. The date was the 18th too, 18 being 6 + 6 + 6, and I suspected that both 216 and 18 were shorthand for the number of the beast. A '666' had been woven into my angelic encounters, as I recounted in chapter 1, and I now sensed that I was close to understanding something important about it. At the time I was listening to *The Orchestral Tubular Bells*, an orchestral transcription by David Bedford of Mike Oldfield's *Tubular Bells*. I looked at the front cover, which featured a tubular bell bent into a triangle, with a partly blue background. Then it hit me: *Tubular Bells* was used as background music in *The Exorcist*, the most famous horror film ever made. And *The Exorcist* was set in

Georgetown, Washington DC, just across the Potomac River from the Pentagon. *The Exorcist* was, of course, the story of the demonic possession of a young girl (who is eleven years old when the Devil enters her) and her eventual release through the rite of exorcism, and its centerpiece was the exorcists' titanic struggle against the Devil. Was this a clue about the meaning of 9/11? Were we possessed by a force that required the power of Christ to remove it?

As I became more sensitive to signs and symbols that might relate to 9/11, I soon began to notice that many movies created around the time of 9/11 appeared to have been influenced by it, even those that were released well before that day. The movie *Ocean's Eleven* (2001) was one of the first I noticed, but I quickly spotted several others. In *Harry Potter and the Philosopher's Stone* (2001), Harry was taken to Hogwarts on his eleventh birthday. *The Two Towers* (2002), the second of the film adaptations of the *Lord of the Rings* trilogy, featured two huge dark towers in the lands of Isengard and Mordor. In *The Matrix* (1999), Neo, a Christ-like figure, is first seen when he opens the door to his apartment, numbered 101. Freakishly, the morning after I watched this movie I passed Keanu Reeves in an Edinburgh street, looking like he had just walked off the set of *The Matrix*, dressed as Thomas Anderson. We were the only two people in the vicinity. It was August, so he was probably there for the Edinburgh Festival, but it was only the third or fourth time in my life I had been that close to anyone famous and I suspected it was another sign.

These movies were all huge blockbusters, reaching mass audiences. If they had been encoded then these were signs for all to see. Intrigued by what I'd found I began to examine popular movies and works of literature from the last fifty years or so, and was amazed to find similar references to 9/11 in many of them. As with the movies released around 2001, most had one overarching theme, a titanic struggle between the forces of light and those of darkness.

Mervyn Peake's imaginative masterpiece *Titus Groan* (1946) begins with the birth of Titus, the 77th Earl of Gormenghast, on the eighth day of the eighth month (8/8). Gormenghast is an ancient, crumbling castle, from which protrudes the immense Tower of Flint. Life in the castle is filled with endless, stultifying ritual, but Titus's birth sees the beginning of unprecedented destruction and change, at the hands of an ambitious kitchen boy. The book was published 55 years before 9/11.

In George Orwell's prescient, dystopian novel *Nineteen Eighty-Four* (1948), London is dominated by four sinister, monolithic towers, from where the totalitarian government of Airstrip One ruthlessly controls and manipulates its citizens. Would-be revolutionary Winston Smith is taken to one of them and finally broken in room 101.

In Alfred Hitchcock's classic suspense movie *The Birds* (1963), the birds begin attacking *en masse* on the eleventh birthday of Mitch Brenner's sister.

The Omen (1976) is an apocalyptic tale about the rise of the antichrist, whose name is Damien Thorn. Amazingly, 'Damien Thorn' and 'antichrist' both have an ordinal value of 121 (11 x 11).

Quatermass and the Pit (1967), called *Five Million Years to Earth* in the US version, is a sci-fi movie about the discovery of a space-craft underground in an area of London long associated with the Devil. The craft contains the bodies of Martians who, Quatermass discovers, had been genetically altering our remote ancestors so that they would periodically cull the population. The killer instinct it controlled was somehow activated by the unearthing of the spacecraft, so that the residents of London who had the gene went on a murderous rampage. The energy of hate manifested as a giant, two-horned head that hovered over the streets of London – much as the twin towers stood over New York – until Quatermass dissipated its energy.

When watching *The Naked Gun* (1988), I was amazed to see

that angels and the number four were brought together in a critical scene, where a remote-controlled baseball player tries to kill the Queen. The would-be assassin plays for the LA Angels and his jersey is number 44 (11 x 4). Interestingly, Osama bin Laden was 44 years old on 9/11/01.

This number also features at the climactic ending of *Dirty Harry* (1971), where Harry Callaghan speaks the famous line about his Magnum 44 being 'the most powerful handgun in the world'. Callaghan throws away his badge after the final shoot-out with the serial killer. The identification number on the badge is 2211 (11 x 201).

In the classic sci-fi film *The Day the Earth Stood Still* (1951), an alien called Klaatu lands his spaceship in Washington DC to warn us that man's warlike nature and his development of atomic rockets are a threat to other planets, therefore Earth may have to be destroyed. Klaatu decides to give mankind a warning and briefly considers the possibility of leveling New York or sinking the Rock of Gibraltar, both actions resonating with what occurred on 9/11. Interestingly, Klaatu was deliberately modeled on Jesus Christ: after being shot he is 'resurrected' by his robot, Gort, and he also adopts the pseudonym of 'Mr. Carpenter'.

In *2001: A Space Odyssey* (1968), in the year 2001 an alien artifact in the form of a large rectangular monolith is discovered buried underneath the Moon's surface. This is identical to one previously found by our early human ancestors. The discoveries of these monoliths are related to important steps in human development.

In *Close Encounters of the Third Kind* (1977), the aliens reveal themselves at a natural monolith called Devil's Tower, in Wyoming. The movie's main character, played by Richard Dreyfuss, has psychic visions of the tower, becomes obsessed with it and sculpts it in his kitchen, before recognizing the object of his visions on a TV news story and eventually making his way there to meet the visitors.

In *Highlander* (1985), antique dealer Russell Nash is one of a group called the Immortals, who come to New York to compete for The Prize, which is essentially the ability to read the thoughts of others. The only way to defeat an opponent is to cut off his head, which is close to what happened to the twin towers on 9/11, since the attacking planes both struck near the top of each tower. Once again there is evil to be faced, this time in the figure of Kurgan.

Independence Day (1996) concerns the invasion of Earth by a fleet of large alien spaceships, which hover over our cities. The invasion is stopped by a successful suicide attack on the huge mothership, made by one of the defending fighter pilots. Just as he launches the attack he speaks the immortal words: 'Hello, boys. I'm back!' Beside his head the number 440 can be seen on the wall of his cockpit. 440 is a multiple of 11 and the ordinal value of 'September the Eleventh, Two Thousand and One'.

As I stated earlier, the most famous person to be killed on 9/11 was David Angell, co-creator of the excellent TV comedy *Frazier*. I loved *Frazier*, which ran for eleven series, from 1993 to 2004 (meaning that 2001 was its ninth season). I noticed that Frazier Crane's room number in the Seattle tower block where he lived was 1901.

Having found what seemed to be premonitions of 9/11 in blockbusting movies of the last fifty years or so, I wondered if our lives had been influenced in other ways. I began to look at our wider culture and history to see if they contained any intimations of that future event. Here are some examples of what I found.

The Ninth of Av is a Jewish day of fasting and mourning, when Jews commemorate the many tragedies that have befallen them on that date in history, particularly the destruction of the first and second temples in Jerusalem; these tragedies are seen as signs of God's disapproval of the behavior of his people at the time. Av is the eleventh month of the Jewish calendar, so the Ninth of Av is a '9/11'. In 2001, the Ninth of Av was on 29 July, which was 44 days before 9/11. Traditionally on this day the book of Lamentations is read in the synagogue. In the Bible, each of the five chapters of Lamentations has either 22 or 66 verses.

In 1190 there was an infamous massacre of about 150 Jews in Clifford's Tower in York, at the hands of an angry mob. Some committed suicide, others died after it was set on fire and the rest were murdered. The date, the fact that they died in a tower and the naming of New York after York all resonate with 9/11.[8]

In the UK, Armistice Day, celebrating the ending of World War I, is celebrated on 11 November every year, with two minutes' silence at 11:00 a.m. Interestingly, the word 'November' is derived from the Latin word *novem*, which means 'nine'.

The assassination of President John F. Kennedy took place in Dallas, Texas on 22 November, 1963, the date including an eleven and a multiple of eleven.

In 1965 a huge electricity blackout affected many parts of northeast USA, including New York. This took place on 9 November of that year. The number of days from 11/9/65 to 9/11/01 was 13,090 (11 x 1190).

The uncanny timing of the solar eclipse of 1999, which began as seen from UK soil at 11:11 a.m. on 11 August, could also have been a forewarning of 9/11.

Pope John Paul II, head of the Roman Catholic Church from 1978 to 2005, was the 264th pope, 264 being 11 x 24. He was also the 110th pope from Celestine II to 'the end of the world', according to the prophecies of St. Malachy.

On a more personal note, there was a world-famous UFO encounter only two miles from where I lived at the time, at Dechmont Law, near Livingston, in Scotland. This traumatic event involved a landscape gardener who worked with a friend of mine. He was working alone in some woods one morning when he came upon an unusually shaped aircraft. Two spheres emerged from the craft, rolled towards him (leaving tracks on the ground) and attached themselves to his trousers, ripping two large holes in them and pulling him to the ground. The ripped trousers may have symbolized the future destruction of the twin towers. The date of this encounter, 22 years before 9/11, was 11/9/79.

On Christmas Eve 1992 my wife and I had our own encounter, witnessing a craft of some kind hovering over a local range of hills. We saw it for about five minutes and from different angles, so I can say with certainty that it hovered directly above the highest peak, the precise spot where I used to camp as a teenager. The date this occurred was 2929 (101 x 29) days before the end of the second millennium. Even more bizarrely, our sighting had happened 119 days after another famous Scottish UFO abduction, the A70 Encounter. The two men involved had been driving to the tiny village of two hundred people where my wife and I now live, another unlikely coincidence.

These seemingly related episodes shed a new light on the UFO phenomenon. For believers, UFOs are often viewed as either technologically advanced aliens or as some type of demonic manifestation. However, my interpretation, if correct, suggests that, assuming UFOs exist and whatever their origin may be, even this phenomenon is under God's control.

It turned out that the aftermath of 9/11 was marked with the number eleven in the same way as the lead-up. For instance, the 9/11 Commission Hearings closed on 17 June, 2004, 1010 days after 9/11. *The 9/11 Commission Report* was released on 22 July, 2004, 1045 (11 x 95) days after the event. These could conceivably have been deliberate choices on someone's part, but they also fitted the growing pattern of elevens I have found clustering around 9/11, recent history and popular culture.

The Madrid train bombings of 11 March, 2003 took place on the 1166th day of the third millennium, 1166 being 11 x 106. The train and bus bombings in London on 7 July, 2005 became known in the UK as '7/7', 77 being another multiple of 11.

Another contender for a post-9/11 aftershock was an astronomical alignment, the so-called Harmonic Concordance, of 2003, where the planets in our solar system, observed from Earth, formed the points of a near-perfect hexagon (six-sided figure) in the sky behind our Moon. The 2003 Harmonic Concordance peaked on 11/9/03. It was during the same week as the Harmonic Concordance that I produced my first web page on 9/11. I remember it well because Karen announced out of the blue that she was taking the girls on holiday for a few days. That was completely out of character for her, in fact the first time she had ever gone on holiday without me in over eighteen years of marriage. I was left on my own for almost a week at a time when I desperately needed to work on the page without the usual distractions of family life.

I had a feeling that at a deep level we collectively sensed the approach of the devastating attacks on 11 September, 2001. My own precognitive dreams showed me that my unconscious was aware of future events; that maybe explained why artists and writers, who are more in touch with their unconscious minds than most, could have been influenced by 9/11, just as Richard Dreyfuss's character in *Close Encounters* had been influenced by the future close encounter at Devil's Tower. I couldn't even begin to speculate about how astronomical events could have been influenced, but if events on Earth and in the heavens were echoing 9/11, and our most creative minds had unwittingly encoded 9/11 into their work, what did that say about its importance? The answer to that question, along with many others, was contained in a puzzle I was just about to solve.

Chapter 4

The September-11 Crucifix

When they came to the place called the Skull, they crucified him there, along with the criminals - one on his right, the other on his left.
   Luke 23:33

On 28 December, 2001, I finally became a Christian. I'd gone along to a meeting of the Christian Business Men's Fellowship, the second one I'd attended. At one point in the evening the pastor asked if anyone would like to give their life to Jesus Christ and I suddenly decided to take the leap of faith I'd been considering for a while. A man called Bob stood up too, so Bill and Bob came forward to be baptized into the Holy Spirit, which we all thought was funny and which made for a very light-hearted baptism. I later noticed the way the number two seemed to have been insinuated into the occasion: it was my second BMF meeting, there were two baptisms and our names began with 'B', the second letter of the alphabet.

   Looking back, I can see early signs that I was destined to follow the Way of the Cross. For instance, as a boy I was envious of my Roman Catholic peers, because they received an ash cross on their foreheads on Ash Wednesday, which I thought was cool. You have to be careful what you wish for, though, because I eventually received a cross-shaped scar in the center of my forehead, just above the hairline, when I slipped and hit my head on a stone. The day it happened was Ash Wednesday of that year.

   Even as I began my Christian journey I knew that I had a job to do, so I got to work. At first I continued to look for numbers encoded into 9/11. What I eventually found was a geometric puzzle, the first part of which is shown in this chapter.

One day I worked out the ordinal value of the two structures hit on that day.

The Pentagon (o) = 125
The World Trade Center (o) = 218

The number 125 is 5 x 5 x 5, which was startling, because the Pentagon building is itself associated with the number five: it has five storeys above ground and is constructed in the form of five concentric pentagons (see photograph).

As if that wasn't enough, the word 'pentagon' has a value of 92, which is a pentagonal number!

Later, I discovered that 125 employees of the US Department of Defense had been killed on 9/11.[9] This was all either freakish coincidence or yet more evidence of the unfolding of a higher plan. The builders of the Pentagon no doubt deliberately made it five-sided, with five storeys and five rings, but they couldn't have encoded the English language or decided how many would die that day.

I couldn't see anything significant in the number 218, though. I was stuck and didn't know how to proceed. Then one night after working on these numbers I had a dream: *I am standing outside a pub called the Dovehill Arms. A young girl walks up to me and hands me a gold coin, on which is the number 343. She skips away, trips over, then gets up and skips away again.* The dove is a sign of the Holy Spirit and gold is a symbol of purity and high value, so I knew this dream was important. The girl tripping over suggested the fall of the twin towers.

Next day, I decided to add up the numbers, and that was when I struck gold.

The Pentagon + the World Trade Center (o) = 343

The number 343 is 7 x 7 x 7. So the two structures hit on 9/11 encoded two cubes in their names. 125 (The Pentagon) is the cube of 5, and 218 (The World Trade Center) is the hollow cube that fits round it like a glove to give the cube of 7, with 343 spheres (figure 5).

Figure 5 Cube 125 and Cube 343

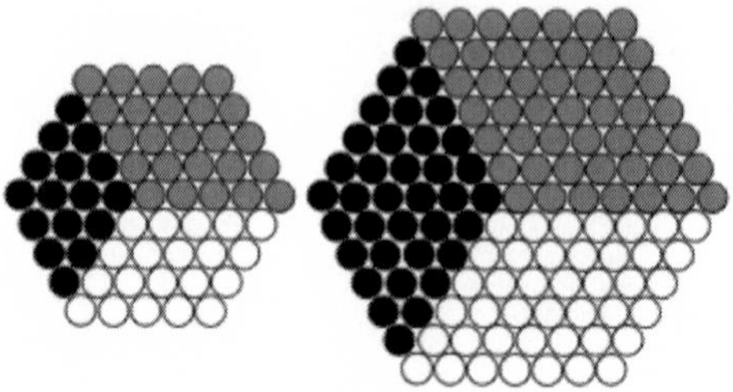

This looked to be as deliberate as the destruction of the towers themselves. But what did it mean? It wasn't immediately obvious to me what that could be. I suspected that it might have something to do with seven, though. Seven is the number of spiritual perfection, the union of spirit (3) and matter (4).

As I look back through my notes I realize with gratitude that I have been helped in my work by many people, from family and friends to work colleagues and perfect strangers. Most of them weren't aware of this guidance; they just played their parts, oblivious to the effect they were having on me. However, the help I got from them was indispensable, confirming my intuitions, giving me a critical piece of information, nudging me in the right direction or letting me know when I was seriously off-course.

One woman in particular I have to thank for passing on a very important dream in 2004, which just had to be confirmation of something I had begun to suspect but didn't yet have enough evidence to believe. She related the following dream to me: *I swap bodies with my cousin, who is very beautiful. My father then catches my cousin (in my body) with a diary in which I have written many hateful things about him. My father reads the diary then attacks my cousin in anger, slashing her back and chopping off two fingers.* It took me an hour or so to realize that this was a dream about 9/11. The two chopped-off fingers represented the destruction of the twin towers, suggesting it was a punishment from God (the father in the dream) for our rebellion (the hateful things written about him). However, the beautiful cousin who took the punishment for my workmate, because they'd swapped bodies, reminded me of the Perfect Sacrifice who took our place on the Cross. The slashes across her back were a reminder of the scourging with whips he received before his crucifixion.

The Crucifixion is first recounted in Matthew 27, so I read through the chapter. By this time I had long been in the habit of looking for numbers that might be encoded alongside the verse, such as the numbers of words and letters, the positional value of the verse and similar numbers, so I kept this in mind as I did so. Then I came to Matthew 27.37: 'Above his head they placed the written charge against him: THIS IS JESUS, THE KING OF THE

JEWS.' The charge against Jesus stopped me in my tracks, because it consisted of eight words and twenty-seven letters, and 8 and 27 are the cubes of 2 and 3. Feeling I was on to something, I worked out the ordinal value:

THIS IS JESUS, THE KING OF THE JEWS (o) = 343

It was the cube of 7 again! Then I noticed that the chapter number was 27, the cube of 3 again, and the sum of the chapter and verse numbers was 64, the cube of 4. This verse was *watermarked* with cubes. It was also the NIV New Testament's 1019th verse, pointing again to a connection between the Crucifixion and 9/11. By luck or God's grace I eventually made that connection, when I learned that if a hollow cube is opened up a certain way, it transforms into a cross.

I had already found a hollow cube, corresponding to the ordinal value of 'The World Trade Center'. Here it is, along with the cross of 218 spheres it forms on opening up (figure 6)

Figure 6 H. Cube/Cross H.Cube/Cross 218

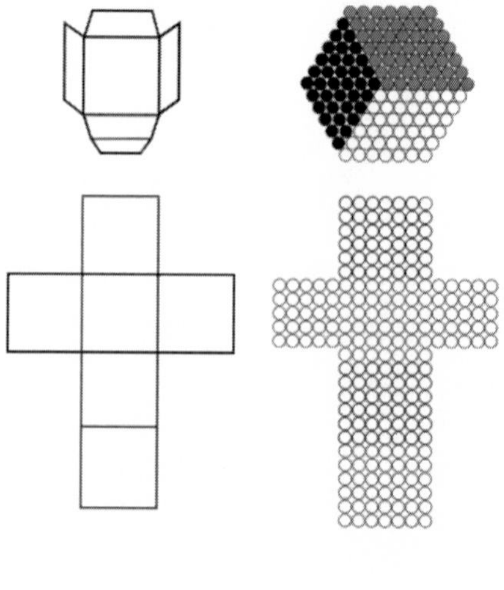

Could the World Trade Center therefore have symbolized the Cross, through its ordinal value of 218? Perhaps the twin towers were the stake and crossbar. I had a growing conviction that I was on the right track, but I needed more evidence to be sure. I looked for further symbolism related to the Crucifixion, turning to the Pentagon.

I knew that the Pentagon had been stamped with the number five, both through its design and through its name and the numbers encoded within it. What then did the number five symbolize? For Christians, five is associated with the five wounds received by Jesus as he was crucified: those to his two wrists, his two feet and his side. In fact, the early Christians used the pentagram as a symbol of the crucified Lord before it was dropped in favor of the cross. In the Bible, five was the number of God's grace and favor. That also seemed to be appropriate for Jesus Christ, as did the fact that in Judaism the cube is the symbol of perfection.

Further compelling evidence was the fact that the ordinal value of 'Jesus Christ', 151, could be displayed as a centered pentagram (figure 7).

Figure 7 Centred Pentagram 151

In fact the numbers 11 and 911 are also pentagram numbers, part of the same numerical series as 151. I could see that these numbers had been carefully chosen to be part of a web of connecting links between the events of 11 September, 2001, and the figure of Jesus Christ.

Christian symbolism associates the wounds of Christ with the five petals of the wild rose. The rose has long been associated with the number five and its geometry and therefore carries precisely the same symbolic meaning as the pentagon and pentagram. In fact in the well-known emblems of the Freemasons and Rosicrucians, the rose takes the place of Jesus Christ on the Cross.

It was now obvious that the Pentagon, through its associations with five, the rose, Jesus Christ and the Passion, must have symbolized the crucified Lord. Then one day it all crystallized in my mind. I saw that if, instead of opening out hollow cube 218 as before, I opened out the 218 spheres on the surface of cube 343, these became the cross again, but this time cube 125 was automatically positioned where the beams crossed. Thus was revealed a symbolic crucifix, which I call *The September-11 Crucifix* (figure 8).

Figure 8 The September-11 Crucifix

If I was right, then the September-11 Crucifix had been encoded within the 9/11 targets for the purpose of delivering this stunning message to the world: *the terrorist attacks of 11 September, AD 2001, were a reenactment of the Crucifixion of Jesus of Nazareth, in AD 33.* It was enormous conclusion to draw, however, so I continued to hunt for evidence.

One further piece of evidence was the fact that the rose is botanically related to the apple, which displays a pentagram of pips when cut through the center. The apple was a symbol in my childhood dream recounted at the start of this book, where one of the doors had an apple handle. The other city involved in the crucifixion drama, New York, is known as 'The Big Apple'.

Among the 2996 people who died on 9/11 were 343 New York Fire Department firefighters and paramedics (over 10% of the total).[10] They mostly perished during the collapse of the twin towers, many of them still climbing to reach the fires that raged above. Like everyone else I was moved by their bravery and sacrifice. I couldn't help noticing, though, that, since the total number of people who died at the Pentagon was 125, both of the cubes the code used to depict the Crucifixion were reflected in the death tolls.

I searched through the Gospel accounts of the Crucifixion, looking for further links with 9/11. According to John, Jesus was wounded on the cross by a soldier's spear: 'Instead, one of the soldiers pierced Jesus' side with a spear, bringing a sudden flow of blood and water' (John 19.34). The ordinal value of this verse, the only one in the Gospels to describe the incident, forged a stunning link between the wounding of Jesus and 9/11:

Instead, one of the soldiers pierced Jesus' side with a spear, bringing a sudden flow of blood and water. (o) = 911

This suggested to me that the attack on the Pentagon by Flight 77 was nothing less than a reenactment of the piercing of Jesus' side by the soldier's spear.

I found another connection between 9/11 and the Crucifixion in the Roman Catholic tradition. The Stations of the Cross are fourteen depictions of the Passion found in every Roman Catholic church. They begin with Jesus being sentenced to death and end with his burial. Although the number of stations was fixed in 1733 by Pope Clement XII, the eleventh station shows Jesus being nailed to the cross (the word 'crucifixion' is derived from two Latin words meaning 'cross' and 'fix').

The Gospels also tell us that two criminals were crucified alongside Jesus, and I wondered how they might have been represented in the 9/11 drama. All the Gospels mention the criminals, but Luke's version is marked with eleven, because the passage is found in Luke 23.32 and 2332 is 11 x 212. I worked out the value of the verse itself:

Two other men, both criminals, were also led out with him to be executed. (o) = 693 = 11 x 63

This verse was the meeting place, then, of a confluence of elevens. In none of the other three Gospels did either the chapter and verse indicators or the verse itself happen to be a multiple of eleven. But in Luke's version both were, something unlikely to have occurred by accident. It seemed likely that these encoded elevens were marking that verse for our attention, as the letter X (formed from two strokes, like 11) is used on treasure maps.

Verse 33 (11 x 3) was also encoded with elevens:

When they came to the place called the Skull, there they crucified him, along with the criminals – one on his right, the other on his left. (o) = 1210 = 11 x 11 x 10

The marking of these verses in Luke with eleven, the number clustered around the destruction of the twin towers, was indicating that these two temples of mammon represented the two criminals crucified alongside Jesus.

I was now convinced: the September-11 Code was plainly telling us that 9/11 was a staged drama representing the Crucifixion of Jesus Christ. The World Trade Center symbolized the Cross, the Pentagon symbolized the crucified Lord, and the twin towers played the parts of the two criminals crucified either side of him. The ordinal value of 'Jesus Christ', 151, was visually depicting the same idea in fact. The Cross is also traditionally associated with the number four, so the number 444 could also be seen as a reference to the three crosses.

Although it all fitted perfectly, I sweated over this interpretation for a long time, knowing how flaky, and perhaps offensive, it would sound to many people. The dream my work colleague had, about her beautiful cousin taking her punishment for her, went a long way to convincing me I was on the right track, but it was such a big claim to make, I dragged my heels over it, unwilling to proclaim something so controversial without a sign I was doing the right thing. Then I received the following image (figure 9):

Figure 9 The Author's "Ransom" Vision

```
R              R
A              A
N              N
S              S
O              O
M              M
```

In Christian theology, Jesus Christ died as the ransom payment for our sins, replacing, once and for all, the annual sacrificial offerings made by the Israelites. The two vertical words symbolized the twin towers, and the vision was telling me that the towers had also been sacrificed as a ransom payment. I had the confirmation I sought.

God wouldn't be God if he couldn't shock and challenge us, and I could see that 9/11 and the message it delivered were assaults not just on physical buildings but on the beliefs about God and our world held by the majority of people in the west, Christian or otherwise. But then maybe we needed to have them shaken up. Maybe we in the west especially needed to have the protective bubble of comfortable certainties with which we had surrounded our lives pierced, to let the fresh air of reality in. 9/11 certainly achieved that. Like the Crucifixion itself, 9/11 was a watershed moment in history: we now use the terms pre-9/11 and post-9/11 in the same way as we say BC and AD, because we know that our world is now changed forever.

Chapter 5

The Signatures of Christ

For in six days the LORD *made the heavens and the earth, the sea,*
and all that is in them, but he rested on the seventh day.
    Exodus 20.11

As a boy I was fascinated by dinosaurs, so I decided that I would
become a paleontologist when I grew up. That career decision
went the way of most boyhood dreams, but in a way I did
become a kind of fossil hunter. The 'fossils' I discovered were the
numerical patterns laid down within the text of the NIV Bible. I
unearthed them not with hammer and chisel but with a hand-
held calculator and the key I had been given. Like a paleontologist I traced out faint, tell-tale imprints in the text, and isolated
them for further study. And from the fragments I gathered, I
gradually pieced together the structure of the strange and
magnificent creature that lay buried within the text.

It occurred to me that other people might have been inspired
to use gematria to look for codes in the Bible, so I scoured the
internet for like-minded souls, but found little apart from tradi-
tional Kabbalah studies (which held no interest for me) and a
growing number of 9/11 conspiracy sites (some of which were of
interest to me - more on that later). One day, however, I came
across the work of a retired mathematics lecturer called Vernon
Jenkins, who claimed to have found geometric figures encoded
within the Hebrew and Greek scriptures, from which the Bible
was compiled.[11] There was nothing on 9/11 or prophecy in his
work but in some ways it was like my own, although rather more
mathematical. I read everything on his website and learned a lot
in the process, including another way of turning words into

numbers.

In classical antiquity, systems of alphabetic numeration abounded. The numerals 1, 2, 3, etc used almost everywhere today were just being invented in India, and the Hebrews, Greeks and other Mediterranean peoples used letters from their alphabets as numerals for counting purposes. The Hebrew system of numeration was structured differently from the ordinal value system I was using, giving much larger values for words and phrases. The first nine letters took the values 1 to 9; the next nine letters took the values 10 to 90; the final four letters took values from 100 to 400. The Greek system was essentially the same. Vernon mentioned in his website that this system, which I call the *standard value*, could in principle be applied to the English alphabet (table 5.1):

Table 5.1 The Standard Value System		
A = 1	J = 10	S = 100
B = 2	K = 20	T = 200
C = 3	L = 30	U = 300
D = 4	M = 40	V = 400
E = 5	N = 50	W = 500
F = 6	O = 60	X = 600
G = 7	P = 70	Y = 700
H = 8	Q = 80	Z = 800
I = 9	R = 90	

I tried it myself on various words and phrases to get a feel for it and quickly realized it was important. At this point I wasn't sure if I was meant to use it, though. But I hadn't reckoned with the key. Since receiving the piece of text that I call 'the key' I had tried in vain to find out how it worked. In fact I wasn't even sure if it was meant to be turned into numbers. The ordinal values of each verse (1 Thessalonians 5.23–24) were 1559 and 468, and the ordinal value of all the words typed (by means unknown) on the bookmark, was 2194. None of these numbers meant anything to me, however. Perhaps the verses were just meant to inspire me to become a Christian.

Then, one day, after working out the standard value of the title 'the Lord God', which was 468, I remembered that this was the same as the ordinal value of the second verse of the key. I quickly looked up the other numbers I'd gotten from the key using the ordinal value system (1559 and 2194), comparing them with lists of standard values I'd compiled – and realized to my surprise that these numbers also made perfect sense under the standard value system. Now I knew exactly how to use the key.

This is how the key works. The ordinal value of each verse is shown again below.

May God himself, the God of peace, sanctify you through and through. May your whole spirit, soul and body be kept blameless at the coming of our Lord Jesus Christ. (o) = 1559
The one who calls you is faithful and he will do it. (o) = 468

These are the standard values of the following titles:

Our Lord Jesus Christ (s) = 1559
The Lord God (s) = 468

Since God and Jesus Christ were referred to in the key, I had little doubt that these were the names the numbers were identifying, especially since 'Our Lord Jesus Christ' was the very title used in the second verse.

The key was indicating that numbers were encoded within the NIV Bible as ordinal values, but took on meaning as standard values. As far as I am aware, this two-stage system is unique to the September-11 Code and it was something I would have been unlikely to arrive at on my own. I now suspect that the code was timelocked, ensuring that the information encoded within the NIV Bible would not be decoded until the time was right. A two-stage system which required a decryption key would be an excellent way of keeping the contents of the code secure until the key was provided. Now it was time to test that system.

I went back to Matthew 27.37, the verse from Matthew's crucifixion narrative describing the charge against Jesus, which I wrote about in the last chapter: 'Above his head they placed the written charge against him: THIS IS JESUS, THE KING OF THE JEWS' (Matthew 27.37). I had discovered that the capitalized words had an ordinal value of 343, the cube of 7, and that other cubes had been encoded there. However, the ordinal value of the entire verse was 826, which meant nothing to me. I reasoned that if this verse really was an important piece of the code, 826 should mean something and the key should unlock that meaning. It turned out that 826 was the standard value of a short phrase that summed up the Crucifixion:

The crucified Lord (s) = 826

So, in this instance at least, both key and code seemed to be validated. Next I went back to the verse in Luke I also showed in the last chapter, relating how two criminals were led out to be executed along with Jesus: 'Two other men, both criminals, were also led out with him to be executed' (Luke 23.32). This had an ordinal value of 693, which was the standard value of another phrase related to the narrative.

The Skull (s) = 693

The Crucifixion had taken place at Golgotha, which Matthew, Mark and John called 'The Place of the Skull'. However, Luke's account named it 'the Skull', which was the very phrase apparently encoded here. Again this two-system decoding process provided a meaningful link between the verse and the larger narrative. The fact that 693 and 2332 are multiples of eleven also linked the crucifixion drama to 9/11, as I showed in the last chapter.

Using the key just like this, I found that many numbers that had puzzled me now made perfect sense. For instance, the standard value of 'Osama bin Laden' was 353, which I now saw had potential meaning within the context of 9/11 being a crucifixion:

Osama bin Laden (s) = 353
Cross (s) = 353

In chapter 3 I wrote that the number 263 often appeared, but that I initially had no idea what it meant. For instance, it was the sum of the three flight numbers on the planes that hit their targets (11, 175 and 77) and the ordinal value of the fullest version of Osama bin Laden's name: Osama bin Muhammad bin Awad bin Laden. With the key I was now able to make sense of the number.

Messiah (s) = 263

The key seemed to be exposing a much deeper level of meaning within 9/11 than any political or sociological analysis had so far uncovered. Osama bin Laden and his four angels of death appeared to be players in a divine production, the script of which was becoming ever more clear to me.

I found more fascinating links to Jesus Christ in the details of 9/11. The twin towers were individually known as the North Tower and the South Tower (these were the names on the architect's plans for the World Trade Center). Using the system I'd learned, I found that these names were not accidental. There are two main spellings for the Hebrew name for Jesus: 'Yehoshua' (consisting of the Hebrew letters Yod, He, Shin, Vav, Ayin) and the shorter 'Yeshua' (Yod, Shin, Vav, Ayin), which has a value of 386.

Yeshua (s, Heb.) = 386
The North Tower + The South Tower (s) = 386

A subtle point I picked up from Judaism may be relevant here. The letter that turns Yeshua into Yehoshua is 'He', the fifth letter of the Hebrew alphabet. Its addition to a name is a sign of divine approval. So Abram became Abraham when he was charged with leading the Israelites out of Egypt. The subtraction of a 'He' suggests the opposite: divine disapproval. This suggested to me that the towers had been marked for destruction.

I added the two flight numbers of the attacks on the WTC to the ordinal values of 'The World Trade Center' and 'New York' and got this number:

11 + 175 + The World Trade Center + New York (o) = 515
Jesus (s) = 515

I tried the same with their equivalents in Arlington County (the Pentagon is situated here, across the Potomac River from Washington DC).

77 + The Pentagon + Arlington County (s) = 410
Christ (s) = 410

This seemed to be compelling evidence of design and again it insisted that Jesus Christ was both the author of and somehow symbolized by these events. I played around with the ordering of these numbers but the only way I could obtain the values of 'Jesus' and 'Christ' was to use the grouping that reflected what actually happened on 9/11. This, along with the appearance of the key in November 2001, again showed that the code had contained a kind of timelock, ensuring that these numbers could not be found, in fact would not exist, until the moment for their revelation.

I now appreciated just how powerful a tool the key was. What I didn't know was where I should look next. But the key itself showed me precisely where. The third number I'd found in the key was the ordinal value of all the words it contained:

> Dear Bill, May God himself, the God of peace, sanctify you through and through. May your whole spirit, soul and body be kept blameless at the coming of our Lord Jesus Christ. The one who calls you is faithful and he will do it. Love Paul (o) = 2194

This is the standard value of the NIV Bible's first verse:

> In the beginning God created the heavens and the earth. (s) = 2194

I took out my NIV Bible and started from the beginning. First I simply worked out the ordinal values of the first few words to see if I came across the standard values of any related words or phrases. It wasn't long before I again found the number 515, this time stamped on the NIV Bible's first twelve words.

> In the beginning God created the heavens and the earth. Now the (o) = 515
> Jesus (s) = 515

The number twelve was also significant. According to Bullinger, it represents perfect government and was both the number of Jesus' disciples and the tribes of Israel, so that fitted too. I wondered if there might be a continuing pattern of twelves, so I worked out the ordinal value of the next twelve words:

> earth was formless and empty, darkness was over the surface of the (o) = 654
> Word (o) = 654

The Word is introduced in John's Gospel: 'In the beginning was the Word, and the Word was with God, and the Word was God' (John 1.1, NIV). John later tells us that Jesus Christ is the Word made flesh.

I had discovered the first two examples of the phenomenon I call *The Signatures of Christ*: six numerical 'signatures' encoded within the first twenty-four words of the NIV Bible. The signatures are revealed simply by cutting the twenty-four words into four consecutive strings of six words (table 5.2)

Table 5.2 The Signatures of Christ in Genesis 1:1-2 (NIV)			
In the beginning God created the (6 words)	*heavens and the earth. Now the* (6 words)	*earth was formless and empty, darkness* (6 words)	*was over the surface of the* (6 words)
o.v. = 252	o.v. = 263	o.v. = 391	o.v. = 263
Jesus		Word	
	Messiah	Yehoshua	Messiah
	Word		

What made these encodings, rather than chance occurrences, was the degree of order and structure they displayed. For instance, the six signatures were in three pairings: Jesus/Yehoshua, Word/Word and Messiah/Messiah. Another indication of design was the unifying presence of the number six, an obvious reference to the six working days of Creation, which is the very subject of the portion of text within which these numbers are encoded.

Every feature of the signatures evidenced that they were genuine encodings and not the kind of random numbers that would be found in any text. There were no gaps between them, no overlaps and no irregular lengths of word string. They were found within the most highly visible words in Scripture, beginning the Bible's opening book and introducing the Creation account. The Bible as a whole told the story of man's turbulent relationship with God and God's eventual reconciliation with Creation through the sacrifice of his Son. Seen in this light, the most impressive feature of these signatures was that they identified the signatory as Jesus Christ.

I was also swayed by the fact that the basic elements of the signatures – the location, the ordinal values, the string lengths – were independent of each other. The chances of them simply coming together, therefore, was effectively nil. But they had come together, nevertheless, forming a perfectly integrated matrix of meaningful numbers where none should be.

The total number of words in the four consecutive strings was twenty-four. This turned out to be a significant number too, effectively tying these encodings together. A third widely used system of numerating words, called the *reduced value*, removes all the zeros from the standard values, giving values of 1 to 9 for all the letters of the alphabet (table 5.3).

Table 5.3 The Reduced Value System		
A = 1	J = 1	S = 1
B = 2	K = 2	T = 2
C = 3	L = 3	U = 3
D = 4	M = 4	V = 4
E = 5	N = 5	W = 5
F = 6	O = 6	X = 6
G = 7	P = 7	Y = 7
H = 8	Q = 8	Z = 8
I = 9	R = 9	

This system gave a value of 24 for both the Greek word 'Ihsous' (Jesus) and the English 'Word':

Ihsous (r, Gr.) = 24
Word (r) = 24

So Jesus and Word were implied again.

After I included the reduced value system in my armory, I found that many previously puzzling numbers suddenly made sense. For instance, I quickly discovered a very compelling explanation for why 9/11 had been so profoundly marked with the number eleven: it was the reduced value of 'Jesus':

Jesus (r) = 11

According to Bullinger, eleven is the number of disorganization, disorder, imperfection and disintegration,[12] which may seem to be at odds with Jesus' supposedly sinless nature. But Jesus 'was numbered with the transgressors' (Luke 22.37) while incarnated, and 'bore our sins in his body on the tree' (1 Peter 2.24). So it fitted that his name should be marked with the number eleven and that this number should have clustered around the event that portrayed his crucifixion.

While working on the signatures, I found the standard value of 'Jesus' and 'Christ' encoded there too, and in a way that again linked Jesus Christ with 9/11. Starting from the beginning of Genesis then numerating strings of seven, nine and eleven words (the first three terms in the simple numerical series 7, 9, 11, 13 ...) gave the standard values, as usual, of 'Christ' and 'Jesus' for the nine- and eleven-word strings (table 5.4).

Table 5.4 Jesus Christ as a '9-11' in Genesis 1.1-2 (NIV)		
In the beginning God created the heavens (7 words)	and the earth. Now the earth was formless and (9 words)	Empty, darkness was over the surface of the deep and the (11 words)
	o.v. = 410	o.v. = 515
	Christ	Jesus

Bearing in mind that 11 is the reduced value of 'Jesus', I thought it was also significant that the standard value of the same name was encoded over eleven words.

I began to feel like a diamond miner, using the key to drill into the rockface of the NIV Bible. The opening few words in particular were sparkling with minerals, and another gem I found was a direct reference to all three systems of numeration, hidden in the positioning of the word 'God' in the first three verses of the NIV Bible. Each verse refers to God once, as shown.

[1]In the beginning **God** created the heavens and the earth.
[2]Now the earth was formless and empty, darkness was over

the surface of the deep, and the Spirit of **God** was hovering over the waters. [3]And **God** said 'Let there be light', and there was light.

(Genesis 1.1–3, emphasis added)

'God' is the 4th word, the 30th word and the 37th word in the NIV Bible.

4 + 30 + 37 = 71
God (s) = 71

'God' is also the 4th word in verse 1, the 20th word in verse 2 and the 2nd word in verse 3.

4 + 20 + 2 = 26
God (o) = 26

So these two encodings independently verified the very two numeration systems suggested by the key. The third system was verified by the number of letters to the end of the first 'God', 17. This is the reduced value of 'God'.

I had read Michael Drosnin's *The Bible Code*, several years before my own involvement with a Bible code, after a work colleague handed it to me one day and recommended I read it. At the time I was not a Christian but I thought it was at least possible that a benevolent higher power, existing beyond time and space, could forsee pivotal events in our future. It might then wish to encode them within our holy books for our guidance.

In this type of code, called an equidistant letter sequence (ELS) code, words and phrases are encoded within the text by separating their constituent letters from each other. This would render them undetectable to the reader of the text. The message could only be decoded by knowing the number of letters from one encoded letter to the next (the 'skip interval', which is always the same between each letter of information thought to be encoded). The search for ELS codes usually requires a computer, because the skip intervals are often huge. But a manual search can be carried out within small chunks of text, because the skip intervals would also be small. A small, manageable piece of text was exactly what I had in front of me in the first twenty-four words of the NIV Bible, so I searched within it for ELS codes.

The first possible ELS code I noticed was the word 'God' at a skip interval of 8, within the very first verse (table 5.5).

Table 5.5 "God" Encoded Within Genesis 1:1 (NIV)
InthebeginningGodcreatedtheheave
12345678123456781234567812345678

The implied 888 was interesting, because this was the standard value of 'Ihsous' ('Jesus' in Greek):

Ihsous (s, Gr.) = 888

I created a grid just like the ELS code grids. This one was only eight letters wide but it hid a perfect little cross, right at the start of the NIV Bible (table 5.6).

Table 5.6 ELS Code in Genesis 1:1 (NIV)
Skip Interval: 8
....Inth ebeginni ngGodcre atedtheh eavensan dtheeart

This encoding in particular supported the Christian assertion that Jesus Christ was God Incarnate, linking the three ideas of God, the Cross and Jesus Christ.

Looking at all that I'd found so far in the opening verse of Genesis, I marveled that so much information could be encoded in so few words, especially when I remembered that the NIV was a translation of words already written in another language and the verse had to make grammatical sense. The translators didn't have much to work with, which meant that neither did the encoder.

I told one or two others about this new development. One was a fellow researcher, Gary val Tenuta, who found an identical cross in John 1.1 (table 5.7).

Table 5.7 ELS Code in John 1:1-2 (NIV)
Skip Interval: 29
Inthebeginnin**g**wasthewordandth ewordwaswith**God**andthewordwasG O**d**HewaswithGodinthebeginning.

The skip interval this time was 29, the reduced value of 'Messiah'. Moreover, John's opening words reflected those of Genesis ('In the beginning ...'). These were the first verses of each book and each location was marked with identical crosses. Just perfect.

Greatly encouraged by these finds, I continued searching for ELS codes in the first twenty-four words of Genesis and eventually found a stunning matrix, apparently identifying the Creator of the September-11 Code (table 5.8).

Table 5.8 ELS Code in Genesis 1:1-2 (NIV)
Skip Interval: 29
Inthebeginning**Godcreated**thehe avensandtheearthn**o**wtheearthwa sformlessandempty**d**arknesswaso verthesurfaceof**th**edeepandthes piritofgodwashoveringoverthew

The skip interval was again 29, the reduced value of 'Messiah'. Later, I noticed an incredible correlation between these ELS codes and the Signatures of Christ. What I found was that each of the letters of the word 'code' came from one of the six-word strings within which the signatures were found. The most impressive part of this correlation was that the last letter of 'code' was also the last letter of the signatures. This tied it all together perfectly, showing that the signatures were no fluke but part of a carefully designed watermark stamped on the first few verses of the NIV Bible.

Early on, I considered trying to figure out the odds against these patterns forming randomly, so I could be sure that the winds of chance alone could not have blown them there. I didn't have the expertise to do more than the simplest calculations, but those I did were encouraging.

I picked seventy English words used in the Bible for Jesus, such as Jesus, Lord, Word, Friend, Comforter, etc. Then I worked out their standard values and did a binomial calculation to work out how many of them should have been found in regular strings within the NIV Bible's first twenty-four words. There should have been none, or perhaps one with a bit of luck. In reality there were five (I didn't include Yehoshua, because it is Hebrew and involving another language would complicate the calculations). This should have happened on only 1 in 1200 occasions.

That didn't take into account the fact that the numbers comprising the Signatures of Christ were the values for Jesus, Word and Messiah, three of the most strongly linked to Jesus Christ. If it had been Friend, Shepherd and Counselor I wouldn't have thought it significant myself. When I reduced the list to twenty of the most commonly used English words for Jesus (and Jesus, Word and Messiah would be high up in that list too) the odds shot up to 1 in 50,000 against this happening by chance. Nor did these tests take into account that the name at the top of any such list, Jesus, was the first one encoded, or the meaningful connection between Jesus Christ and the Bible, or the significance of the number six to the Creation story, or the other encodings I found there, adorning the Signatures of Christ like jewels on a crown.

Although the results from these and other tests I did clearly showed that the code was statistically improbable, I eventually abandoned attempts to use statistics as evidence that the code was real. This was because I came to the realization that the code was based on something probability calculations couldn't really measure: *meaning*. Only human minds could decide what was meaningful and what was not and therefore whether the code was no more real than a face in the clouds, or the finger of God himself pointing through them.

Chapter 6

The Beast

Then I saw another beast, coming out of the earth. He had two horns like a lamb, but he spoke like a dragon.
Revelation 13.11

God can be a hard teacher at times. My dreams and visions faithfully reflected my state of mind, but this often felt like a curse rather than a blessing. When my thoughts took a darker turn I would frequently see them displayed before me in all their awful glory. I was also shown the destructive consequences of what I had imagined to be my private broodings and the actions that stemmed from them.

When my thoughts or behavior were seriously off-course I would visit hell worlds in my dreams. This one was particularly vivid: *Something like a porthole or magnifying glass appears in my field of vision. Looking through it, I see a vast cityscape filled with rows of the most run-down dwellings imaginable. I could easily topple one with a good shove. I am given a sweeping view of the entire, dreary scene, then the view zooms in on one of these decaying, surely derelict, hovels. I see to my surprise that it is inhabited. Then I am shown a huge creature that sits atop one of the houses, calmly surveying the entire scene. This realm belongs to it. The creature is vaguely simian but has the wings of a bat or pterodactyl. It wears a fez on its head.* The fez seemed out of place in this Boschian scene, but I knew that every detail in dreams is significant and eventually realized that the word 'fez' has the same ordinal value as 'hell' (37).

The trouble was that I was conflicted. Although I was trying hard to live this new Christian life I'd been given, old patterns of thought and behavior still exerted a pull on me. In addition, although the Holy Spirit had healed me of my most severe problem – my endless, destructive obsessing over my relationship with my old supervisor – I nursed a seemingly endless list of lesser hurts, frustrations and regrets. I knew I was going to have to release these feelings and take more responsibility for my thoughts and actions in future. I had tried and failed to achieve that release on my own in the past, but now I had a powerful ally in the Holy Spirit and I gradually learned to call on him whenever I got too angry or upset.

I also had to be careful not to open up to spiritual influence while I was in the wrong frame of mind. One night, feeling a little depressed, I decided to meditate even though I knew it wasn't a good idea at that time. Soon after I began to meditate I saw with my inner vision a thin, yellowish creature coming towards me. It had a predatory look on its skeletal face. I watched it approach me, observing it with interest but no fear. Suddenly, there was a tremendous flash of light from above and the thing was gone. Afterwards, I realized that, while I had sat there like a hypnotized rabbit, someone much wiser had smelled trouble and intervened. I thanked God for protecting me and gave up meditating for the evening. Spiritual attacks such as this one were rare, but at least gave me an awareness of the reality of the demonic, a concept I would have dismissed as medieval superstition a few years beforehand.

Some of the signs I'd received during my spiritual crash course a few years earlier had brought the number 666 to my attention. From a plethora of signs and synchronicities, such as those I'd found in movies released around 9/11, I was already convinced that this tragedy was related to the eternal struggle between good and evil, but the signs involving 666 had given 9/11 a biblical dimension and further hinted that it may even have been a kind of exorcism. So I decided it was time to grab the beast by its horns, so to speak.

Earlier, I stated that the code uses shorthand versions of the number 666 on occasion. One of them is 216, or 6 x 6 x 6. The other is 18, which is 6 + 6 + 6. Eighteen is the number of the most infamous verse in the Bible: 'This calls for wisdom. If anyone has insight, let him calculate the number of the beast, for it is man's number. His number is 666' (Revelation 13.18). According to Bullinger, six is the number representing man in opposition to God (although it also stands for the work of Creation) and the triple six is the highest expression of man's rebellion.[12] Of course, I couldn't resist the temptation to numerate Revelation 13.18, which turned out to be a Pandora's box of diabolical digits.

The first encoded number I found was over the entire verse (note that the digits of 666 are added like letter values in a word, as if they are fff):

This calls for wisdom. If anyone has insight, let him calculate the number of the beast, for it is man's number. His number is 666. (o) = 1151
Beelzebub (s) = 1151

Once again gematria was mediating a hidden connection between the theme of the verse and a related name. This was especially significant because 'Beelzebub' (NIV spelling) is a name Jesus used for the Devil throughout the Gospels. In my researches I had found that only around one word in a thousand-would have a standard value of 1151, and no other biblical name or title of which I am aware, so either I was uncovering an amazingly unlikely sequence of coincidences or there really was an alphanumerical code buried here. Coincidence was a laughably weak explanation, however, given the regularity with which I was striking gold with the decoding method I had been taught and the immense significance of the passages I was finding to be encoded. It was far more reasonable to accept that the NIV Bible (and 9/11) really did contain an intelligently-designed code. I noted again that the number was encoded as an ordinal value but took on meaning as a standard value, just as the key had shown me.

Full stops split the verse into three sentences, the second of which has three clauses, divided by commas. I found more encoded numbers within these clauses.

let him calculate the number of the beast (o) = 352
Satan (s) = 352

for it is man's number (o) = 216
6 x 6 x 6 = 216

Several encodings in this verse hinted at a relationship between the beast and 9/11. For instance, the last twenty words of the verse had an ordinal value of 911.

anyone has insight, let him calculate the number of the beast, for it is man's number. His number is 666. (o) = 911

The number eighteen seemed to have been stamped on this verse; it was the verse number and also the number of letters in each of the first three groups of four words (two of which were clauses in their own right). Noticing this pattern, I numerated the first eighteen words and found the standard value of the name bin Laden reportedly began using after 9/11: Osama bin Muhammad bin Laden.

This calls for wisdom. If anyone has insight, let him calculate the number of the beast, for it (o) = 848
Osama bin Muhammad bin Laden (s) = 848

In addition, I found 'the Serpent' encoded within the first fifteen words of this same string (table 6.1).

Table 6.1 The Serpent within Revelation 13:18 (NIV)	
This calls for wisdom. If anyone has insight, let him calculate the number of the beast, for it (18 words)	is man's number. His number is 666. (7 words)
Osama bin Muhammad bin Laden	
The Serpent	

I found the value of 'Osama bin Laden' in another remarkable encoding, this time over the third of three eight-word strings (table 6.2).

Table 6.2 Three Encodings within Revelation 13:18 (NIV)		
This calls for wisdom. If anyone has insight, (8 words)	let him calculate the number of the beast (8 words)	for it is man's number. His number is (8 words)
The fallen angel	Satan	Osama bin Laden

The three eights implied 888, standard value of 'Ihsous', implying that although the terrorist attacks on 9/11 were at the human level acts of great wickedness, these actions may have had divine approval.

Another persuasive piece of evidence was the position of Revelation 13.18 in the NIV Bible: it was the NIV Bible's 30,911th verse and the NIV New Testament's 7766th (11 x 706, or 22 x 353). This second number had 11 and 353 (Osama bin Laden) as factors. So 9/11 was indelibly stamped on the Bible's most infamous verse and number.

* * *

Although it's not widely known outside Christian and Jewish circles, the number 666 is actually found in other places within the Bible. In Ezra 2 it is given in a list numbering the men of the families of Israel who returned from exile in Babylon. I suspected that 666 might be a little beacon put in there, so I did a few calculations, which confirmed that I'd stumbled into another one of the beast's lairs.

Here, from verses 3 to 20, are the first eighteen names in the list of exiles – after this there is a break, so these eighteen names stand on their own (table 6.3).

Verse	Family	Count
	Table 6.3 Ezra's List of Returning Exiles (First 18)	
3	Parosh	2172
4	Shephatiah	372
5	Arah	775
6	Pahath-Moab	2812
7	Elam	1254
8	Zattu	945
9	Zaccai	760
10	Bani	642
11	Bebai	623
12	Azgad	1222
13	**Adonikam**	**666**
14	Bigvai	2056
15	Adin	454
16	Ater	98
17	Bezai	323
18	Jorah	112
19	Hashum	223
20	Gibbar	95

Counting down the list, I noticed that the Adonikam were the 11th name. In addition, the tally of the first eleven numbers (to 666) was 12,243 (11 x 1113). This was the only one of the subtotals to be a multiple of eleven, which made it even more impressive.

The next book, Nehemiah, contains an almost identical list of returning exiles. However, there are slight differences in the accounting and the names. Atheists have pointed to such irregularities as evidence that the Bible was purely the work of fallible man, but I found clear evidence that the hand of God was responsible for everything in the Bible and so-called mistakes were often clues to deeper layers of truth.

The most obvious difference between the two lists was Nehemiah's total for the Adonikam of 667, against Ezra's 666. However, when I subtracted Ezra's counts from Nehemiah's, I found a possible reason for the differences Both lists are shown together below, with the last column giving the difference between the counts in Nehemiah and those in Ezra (table 6.4).

Nehemiah 7	Count	Ezra 2	Count	Difference
Parosh	2172	Parosh	2172	0
Shephatiah	372	Shephatiah	372	0
Arah	652	Arah	775	-123
Pahath-Moab	2818	Pahath-Moab	2812	6
Elam	1254	Elam	1254	0
Zattu	845	Zattu	945	-100
Zaccai	760	Zaccai	760	0
Binnui	648	Bani	642	6
Bebai	628	Bebai	623	5
Azgad	**2322**	**Azgad**	**1222**	**1100**
Adonikam	667	Adonikam	666	1
Bigvai	**2067**	**Bigvai**	**2056**	**11**
Adin	655	Adin	454	201
Ater	98	Ater	98	0
Hashum	328	Bezai	323	5
Bezai	324	Jorah	112	212
Hariph	112	Hashum	223	-111
Gibeon	95	Gibbar	95	0

Table 6.4 Differences in Count Between Ezra and Nehem.

Interestingly, the Adonikam were flanked with the numbers 1100 and 11. If eleven really was the marker for 9/11-related encodings then 9/11 was again being linked to the number of the beast. I also discovered that the sum of the numbers of the Azgad and Bigvai given in the two books was a multiple of eleven.

$$2322 + 2067 + 1222 + 2056 = 7667 \ (11 \times 697)$$

I tried summing all the numbers in the two lists, checking the running total at each verse to see if it was a multiple of eleven. What I found was a dazzling pattern of encoded elevens (table 6.5).

Table 6.5 Pattern of Elevens in the Summed Counts			
Nehemiah	Ezra	Running Total	Multiple of 11?
2172	2172	4344	No
372	372	5088	No
652	775	6515	No
2818	2812	12145	No
1254	1254	14653	No
845	945	16443	No
760	**760**	**17963**	**11 x 1633**
648	642	19253	No
628	**623**	**20504**	**11 x 1864**
2322	1222	24048	No
667	666	25381	No
2067	2056	29504	No
655	**454**	**30613**	**11 x 11 x 11 x 23**
98	98	30809	No
328	**323**	**31460**	**11 x 11 x 260**
324	112	31896	No
112	223	32231	No
95	95	32421	No

Yet again the Adonikam and 666 are framed by the number 11, this time as a factor (in some cases double or triple factor) of the running totals at the 7th, 9th, 13th and 15th names. This was the third cluster of encoded elevens and the second symmetrical pattern, all with 666 in the center. It was for me final confirmation of the reality of the September-11 Code. A summary of all the encoded elevens, showing the impressive visual pattern they form, is shown in table 6.6.

Table 6.6 Elevens Encoded Around the Adonikam in Ezra				
Ezra's Counts	Place	Running Total	Running Total Ezra + Nehem.	Family Counts Nehem. - Ezra
2172	1	2172	4344	0
372	2	2544	5088	0
775	3	3319	6515	-123
2812	4	6131	12145	6
1254	5	7385	14653	0
945	6	8330	16443	-100
760	7	9090	**11x1633**	0
642	8	9732	19253	6
623	9	10355	**11x1864**	5
1222	10	11577	24048	**1100**
666	**11**	**11x1113**	25381	1
2056	12	14299	29504	**11**
454	13	14753	**11x2783**	201
98	14	14851	30809	0
323	15	15174	**11x2860**	5
112	16	15286	31896	212
223	17	15509	32231	-111
95	18	15604	32421	0

I had seen a thousand-year-old copy of Ezra with exactly the same numbers and had little reason to doubt they were unchanged since they were recorded. So, incredible as it seems, the code I was finding must have been accumulating within Scripture from the time the first scribes put pen to parchment. The background story of this section of Ezra and Nehemiah is the return of exiled Hebrews from captivity in Babylon; this theme of release from oppression threw an interesting light on the possible meaning of 9/11.

* * *

Diana Gallovich, an ordained minister and the owner of the Eighth Day Assembly website,[13] impressed upon me the importance of the story in Ezra of Tattenai, a Persian governor during the reign of King Darius. Tattenai was foremost among those who opposed the rebuilding of the temple in Jerusalem by the returned captives from Babylon. When the work began, Tattenai and others sent a letter to King Darius asking that a search be made for a document that would validate the claims of the Jews who were rebuilding the temple that this work had been decreed by King Cyrus I, the ruler who had released them from captivity. A document authorizing the rebuilding was found, so King Darius wrote back, ordering that the work was to go on, with financial help from the region Tattenai governed. Anyone who hindered the work was to be impaled on a beam from their own house, which would thereafter be torn down. After that, Tattenai (quite understandably) worked diligently to assist in the rebuilding of the temple.

The story is told in a short section of Ezra (4.8 to 6.18) that is one of the very few parts of the Old Testament written in Aramaic, a language related to Hebrew and the one Jesus spoke. In fact the Aramaic section begins at Ezra 4.8 and ends at 6.18. Adding the two numbers implied by the first and last verses we obtain

$$48 + 618 = 666$$

The first verse in which Tattenai is mentioned is Ezra 5.3 and the final verse is Ezra 6.13. Adding the numbers again gives us

$$53 + 613 = 666$$

Even the English translation of the name is marked with this number:

Tattenai (s) = 666

Since I was by now convinced that 666 and 9/11 were intertwined, I found it difficult to resist the notion that the World Trade Center and Pentagon were together a type of Tattenai. They were a stumbling block to the reinstitution of God's kingdom on earth, standing in opposition to God. Darius's warning in his decree that anyone who opposed the rebuilding work would be impaled on a beam from his house, which would then be pulled down, was symbolically enacted on 9/11.

I found a similar story in Nehemiah. Nehemiah 4.3 quotes the mocking words spoken by Tobiah the Ammonite to the Jews as they were rebuilding the Jerusalem wall: 'Tobiah the Ammonite, who was at his side, said, "What they are building – if even a fox climbed up on it, he would break down their wall of stones!"'

I found the mention of a fox fascinating, because the fox is a byword in the New Testament and in common parlance for the Devil. Its standard value was surely another example of how significant numbers had been woven into language.

Fox (s) = 666

I did a little digging around in the Old Testament and found that Nehemiah 4.3 was the third mention of foxes in the Bible. The first and second verses that mention the animal are found in the book of Judges:

> 4So he went out and caught three hundred foxes and tied them tail to tail in pairs. He then fastened a torch to every pair of tails, 5lit the torches and let the foxes loose in the standing corn of the Philistines. He burned up the shocks and standing corn, together with the vineyards and olive groves.
>
> (Judges 15.4–5)

I summed the numbers implied by the three chapter and verse indicators:

154 + 155 + 43 = 352
Satan (s) = 352

So the opposition by Tobiah to the rebuilding of the wall was as firmly stamped with the mark of the beast as that of Tattenai to the rebuilding of the temple. Again both stories had the general theme of the ending of something evil, in this case the overcoming of opposition to the rebuilding of the temple, which represented God's kingdom on earth.

* * *

I had many questions at this stage about the nature of 9/11 and whether it ultimately helped or harmed us. I wasn't sure I was qualified to make a judgment on it either, aware that 9/11 was a huge hot-button issue, guaranteed to polarize opinion, and that much of what had been spoken and written about it would be tainted with prejudice and propaganda. However, in March 2002, while I was lying in my bath thinking about 9/11 and what it really meant, I was helped by a powerful vision. This was an impression of two words, which was so bright that I could perceive it with my eyes open (most of my visions are seen when my eyes are closed). The words were

ARMS AVARICE

These words have eleven letters, the initial letters are AA (11) and the ordinal value is 110; all of this meant that the vision concerned the 9/11 targets. The distribution of letters is also significant: there are four and seven letters in the words, giving 47 (ordinal value of 'beast') and the individual words have values of 51 (demon) and 59 (dragon).

The two words were obvious references to the WTC and Pentagon and they helped me understand why those structures had been targeted. ARMS symbolized the Pentagon, which is the hub of the USA's military operations: its 'force of arms'. AVARICE means 'lust for money' and was an obvious reference to the World Trade Center. The fact that the Pentagon is located near Arlington National Cemetery, the US Marine Corps headquarters and other structures of military significance only heightened the connection. The same was true of the World Trade Center, which was just across the road from Wall Street.

The vision was telling me, in wonderfully elegant style, that the World Trade Center and the Pentagon were, or had become, forces for evil in the world. The World Trade Center represented *global capitalism*, the American-led economic system which now holds the world in its thrall (unsurprisingly, many of the tenants in the twin towers were financial companies). The Pentagon controls the hidden fist behind America's economic policies and represents the military force that all empires need in order to expand.

The vision firmly marked these structures and the forces from which they drew their power with the number eleven. Bullinger stated that eleven was the biblical number of disorganisation, disorder, disintegration and imperfection. Nine was the number of endings, judgment, finality, fruits and suffering.[14] So '9/11' implied the idea of God's judgment on an imperect system: its ending, its just deserts.

Looking through my NIV Bible, I found that passages describing the destruction or casting down of something evil were very often marked with the number eleven, or even nine and eleven together.

Genesis 10.19 is the first verse to mention the cities of Sodom and Gomorrah, which were destroyed by the Lord because they had given themselves over to sin. The story of Sodom and Gomorrah is told in Genesis 19, so the two chapters these cities appear within are 10 and 19 – containing the digits 9, 1 and 1 again.

The story of the Tower of Babel is told over the first nine verses of Genesis 11. God thwarted this overly ambitious building project – the erecting of a tower that 'reaches to the heavens' – by confusing the languages of men.

In Exodus the Lord shows the Egyptians his power by having Moses and Aaron let loose various plagues to defeat their Pharaoh. Exodus 9.11 tells us that Pharaoh's magicians, after being covered with boils, can no longer stand against Moses: 'The magicians could not stand before Moses because of the boils that were on them and on all the Egyptians' (Exodus 9.11). This meaningful and numerically significant verse has an ordinal value of 957 (11 x 87).

In Deuteronomy 20.20 the Lord tells the Israelites that they may cut down trees that do not produce fruit. 'However, you may cut down trees that you know are not fruit trees and use them to build siege works until the city at war with you falls' (Deuteronomy 20.20). The ordinal value of this verse is 1474 (11 x 134). The twin towers, then, were the fruitless trees that were felled.

1 Samuel 17 tells the story of David defeating Goliath with a single slingshot, which knocks his gigantic adversary to the ground. The verse where David fires the fatal shot is 17.49. 1749 is 11 x 159 and chapter 17 is the Bible's 253rd, 253 being 11 x 23. So the twin towers were a type of Goliath: large and powerful but an enemy of God's people.

Isaiah 30.25 warns of a 'day of great slaughter, when the towers fall ...' The chapter and verse numbers can be read as 3025 (11 x 11 x 5 x 5). The elevens confirmed that this was a prophecy of the fall of the twin towers. Double multiples of eleven, incidentally, are much more significant than single multiples, because there is only a 1-in-121 chance of any number being divisible by 121. The other factor is 5, the number associated with the Pentagon.

In Jeremiah 9.11 the Lord threatens the destruction of Jerusalem and other towns, which could be seen as a prophecy of 9/11:

I will make Jerusalem a heap of ruins,
    a haunt of jackals;
    and I will lay waste the towns of Judah
    so that no-one can live there.

The verse is marked not just by its chapter and verse indicators, but by its ordinal value of 1122 (11 x 102).

Jeremiah 51.48 prophesies an attack on Babylon from the north:

'Then heaven and earth and all that is in them
    will shout for joy over Babylon,
    for out of the north:
    destroyers will attack her,' declares the LORD.

The ordinal value of this verse is 1386 (11 x 126). 5148 is 11 x 468.

In a passage prophesying the destruction of the whole world, Zephaniah 1.16 specifically mentions an attack on the 'corner towers' of Jerusalem:

> ... a day of trumpet and battle cry
> against the fortified cities
> and against the corner towers.

The ordinal value is 847 (11 x 11 x 7).

Revelation 11.3–4 describes the 'two witnesses', which sound suspiciously like the twin towers:

> [3]And I will give power to my two witnesses, and they will prophesy for 1,260 days, clothed in sackcloth. [4]These are the two olive trees and the two lampstands that stand before the Lord of the earth.

Revelation 11.7 describes the destruction of the witnesses: 'Now when they have finished their testimony, the beast that comes up from the Abyss will attack them, and overpower and kill them.' The ordinal value of this verse is 1265 (11 x 115), suggesting that this verse was also a prophecy of 9/11. The beast from the Abyss would seem to be identified with Osama bin Laden and Al Qaeda.

In a passage describing the war in heaven between the angels of light and those of darkness, Revelation 12.9 tells how Satan and his angels were hurled to earth. 'The great dragon was hurled down – that ancient serpent called the devil, or Satan, who leads the whole world astray. He was hurled to the earth, and his angels with him.' The ordinal value is 1518 (11 x 138).

Revelation 13.11 describes the 'beast ... out of the earth' as having 'two horns like a lamb', but speaking 'like a dragon'. The horns were the twin towers, which were blunt like lambs' horns, which meant that this beast was the World Trade Center itself, or rather, the system that gave rise to it.

Revelation 19.20 informs us of the fate of the beast and the false prophet: 'But the beast was captured, and with him the false prophet who had performed the miraculous signs on his behalf. With these signs he had deluded those who had received the mark of the beast and worshipped his image. The two of them were thrown alive into the fiery lake of burning sulphur.' Its ordinal value? 2651 (11 x 241).

Revelation 20.9 describes the destruction of Satan and his followers: 'They marched across the breadth of the earth and surrounded the camp of God's people, the city he loves. But fire came down from heaven and devoured them.' The fate of Satan and the twin towers are conjoined by the elevenness of the verse. The ordinal value is 1342 (11 x 122). 209 is 11 x 19.

These passages and many more in the NIV Bible had been precisely placed and often worded to encode the number eleven, identifying them as nothing less than parables and prophecies of 9/11, around which elevens had also clustered. Although the code was employing many biblical metaphors to aid in our understanding of 9/11, it was steadfast in identifying the World Trade Centre and the Pentagon as the beast, the dragon, the false prophet and Satan. The twin towers, reaching proudly towards the heavens, were the very horns of the beast. *Therefore, the terrorist attacks of 11 September, 2001, were the destruction of the beast, the hurling down to earth of Satan and his angels, the casting of the beast and the false prophet into the fiery lake and the destruction of Satan and his followers.*

The code's identification of the beast is supported by the gematria of the very word 'beast'.

Beast (r) = 11
Beast (s) = 308 = 11 x 28

You may recall from chapter 5 that 'Jesus' also has a reduced value of 11. However, this is because Jesus 'was numbered with the transgressors' (Luke 22.37) while incarnated. The transgressors, of course, are us. At our Godless worst we are indeed beasts, viewing life as a struggle for survival, others as competitors and the Earth's riches and our fellow creatures as resources to be exploited. It was the mindset of the avaricious, power-hungry Henry Potter in the movie *It's A Wonderful Life!* However, as my 'light-bulb' experiences so elegantly demonstrated, this way of life leads to suffering and conflict and thus contains the seeds of its own - and our - destruction: 'If a house is divided against itself that house cannot stand.' (Mark 3.25). The lesson taught me as I struggled with my own conflicts was that we must look to heaven rather than earth for security, meaning and purpose in life and I suspected that 9/11 was the message writ large.

9/11 was the pushing of a reset button on our collective psyche, spellbound by the false prophet of global capitalism and the dragon of consumerism. Although at face value a horrendously evil act, 9/11 symbolized the destruction of a much greater evil. Are surgeons who save a man's life by chopping off two gangrenous fingers committing a criminal act? Is lancing a boil a terrible thing to do? Those gleaming towers, rising proudly above New York – and thus symbolically the entire world – stood for a system of economic imperialism that, like Dr. Frankenstein's monster, the Golem of Jewish fable and the artificial intelligence that had enslaved mankind in *The Matrix*, was now beyond the control of its creators and was threatening to destroy us all.

Despite their rejection of western values, Al Qaeda also had the mark of the beast. Many Muslims believe that the USA in particular – 'the great Satan' – and western capitalism in general are forces inimical to the survival of Islam and that they have a sacred duty, therefore, to attack them. However, in their commitment to violence Al Qaeda were merely a reflection of the worst aspects of the enemy they wished to destroy. This was perhaps why 9/11 and Osama bin Laden were encoded within Revelation 13.18 and why, in Revelation 11.7, the two witnesses were destroyed by the beast from the Abyss.

I couldn't shake off the feeling, though, that bin Laden and the organization he created had been instruments of God on this occasion. The Old Testament is replete with examples of God using Israel's enemies to punish them when they rebelled (for instance, Judges 2.14 and 2 Kings 17.6); I was now sure that 9/11 should be seen in the same light.

Chapter 7

The Manchild

She gave birth to a son, a male child, who "will rule all nations with an iron scepter."
Revelation 12.5.

With my inner vision I would occasionally see a being who was at once very youthful and incredibly ancient. It was childlike in appearance, possessing a grace and purity that was wondrous to behold, yet I also detected a fierce intelligence and a firm sense of mission. At first, the being just observed me from a distance. One time it seemed to be standing on a staircase, about halfway down, watching me with a look of concern. If this was an angel or other spiritual entity, the staircase was probably a symbol for the descent from heaven to earth. Before long, the being began to communicate with me. It spoke quickly and had the voice of a child, yet that voice was somehow charged with wisdom and authority. One day this 'wise child' said something to me that at once identified it and showed me that these communications held more information than I had at first supposed. It said: 'I'm twenty-six and I'm here for you.' 26 is the ordinal value of 'God'. It is also the value of the Hebrew word 'YHVH', the personal name of God and the most sacred word in Judaism. Since the statement appeared to be referencing the numbering of words (it even had 26 letters), it occurred to me to work out its ordinal value:

I'm twenty-six and I'm here for you (o) = 358

Much later, I realized that this was the standard value of the

Hebrew word *Moshiach* (Mem, Shin, Yod, Chet), which means 'Messiah'.

Moshiach (s, Heb.) = 358

This unexpected equivalence between word and phrase was the final proof for me that I wasn't hallucinating these voices, not least because I had received information which I didn't have the knowledge at the time to decode. I had no idea then that the number 358 had any significance and this happened before I'd begun using the standard value scheme of numbering words. Moreover, since I had decoded the message using the same two-part system I was using to crack the code in the NIV Bible, it was reasonable to assume both message and code were from the same source. I felt more than a little awestruck when I contemplated that source, and enormously privileged to be receiving these communications.

Luckily I had written down most of the messages I received, so I could now check them to see if others had been similarly encrypted (they had). I had also gotten into the habit of recording my most vivid dreams and images, partly because I knew they often held answers to code-related problems. One such dream came to me after I'd watched a film called *Pi*, by Darren Aronofsky. It stars Sean Gullette as a brilliant, reclusive, epileptic mathematician called Maximillian Cohen, from New York (of all places), who discovers a 216-digit number that is the key to understanding patterns in nature and human society. I found the film intelligent, entertaining and rather spooky, because I could identify with Max Cohen as few other people could.

A few nights later I had a dream: *From the vantage point of the first floor of my house I see two dogs standing in my back garden, just in front of my garage. They are white with colored patches. I am told that one is my brother-in-law and the other is me. I am also told that this second dog belongs to 'Doctor Cohen'.* On waking up I mulled over the dream and quickly grasped its essential meaning. The garden represented God's Creation, the garage at the end of the garden represented our fallen world, and the position of the dogs next to the garage and their dark patches was a reference to our fallen nature. The inclusion of my brother-in-law in the dream was probably because he lived next door to me at the time. I also saw that the dream had used material from the film *Pi*, because of 'Dr. Cohen'. This name probably symbolized Jesus Christ, because it was Jewish, 'Doctor' represented authority and I was now a Christian, whereas my brother-in-law was not. But I had missed one important point because of my ignorance of Judaism. The surname 'Cohen' is a variant of *Kohan*, a Hebrew word that means 'priest'. For us Christians, Jesus Christ is our High Priest.

One of the areas of theological disagreement between Christians and Jews is that for Christians the Crucifixion ended the need for the Day of Atonement (*Yom Kippur*). The Day of Atonement is the most holy day in the Jewish calendar and falls in late September or early October. Looking through websites on Judaism, I discovered that in 2001 it fell a little after 9/11, on 27 September. Nowadays, Yom Kippur is a day of prayer, fasting and repentance, but little else I found of interest. So I turned to the Bible to find out how the day had been observed when the Jews were desert nomads.

For the ancient Israelites, the Day of Atonement was also the climax of the holy year, but it had far more significance to them. On that day, the High Priest made reparation for the sins of his people through the performance of a sacrificial Rite of Atonement. If God accepted the sacrifice (by no means certain), their sins were forgiven and his covenant with them was renewed for another year. The sacrifices for the Day of Atonement took place in the Tabernacle, a portable temple that was the center of the Israelites' religious life and the basis for the Jerusalem Temple. It was built to precise instructions given in the book of Exodus (figure 10).

Figure 10 The Tabernacle

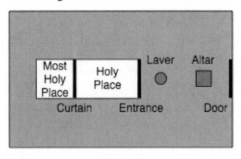

The Tabernacle was simple in structure, consisting of a courtyard and two sanctuaries: the Holy Place and the Most Holy Place. The Holy Place contained a lampstand, showbread table and altar of incense. The Most Holy Place held the Ark of the Testimony (Covenant), and the Ark itself contained the two tablets inscribed with the Ten Commandments, Aaron's staff that budded and the pot of manna. The other major structures were the laver, for washing, and the Altar of Burnt Offering, used for burning offerings to the Lord. The offerings were made daily and also on special holy days, the Day of Atonement being of course the holiest day of all.

Entrance to the Holy Place was reserved for the priesthood and entrance to the Most Holy Place was the exclusive right of the High Priest. Even he could enter only on the Day of Atonement, only after washing and purification, and then only to perform his duties in the Rite of Atonement. The reason for these extreme restrictions on entrance was because the Most Holy Place was the physical location where YHVH, the God of the Israelites, was present among his people. The almost total exclusion of the people from the Most Holy Place symbolized their exiled status and helped to maintain its sanctity.

To enter the Most Holy Place three thresholds had to be crossed:

1. the door to the outer court, separating the Tabernacle

from the outside world;

2. the entrance to the tent, separating the Holy Place from the outer court;

3. the curtain, separating the Most Holy Place from the Holy Place.

Although only the curtain was named as such, all three barriers were curtains.

The Rite of Atonement was performed according to the instructions in Leviticus 16. These required five animals, which would be sacrificed in the following order:

1. A bullock was sacrificed as a sin offering for the High Priest.

2. A young goat was sacrificed as a sin offering for the people.

3. Another young goat, the scapegoat, had the sins of the people laid upon it then was led into the wilderness.

4. A ram was sacrificed as a burnt offering for the High Priest.

5. Another ram was sacrificed as a burnt offering for the people.

After securing the animals and dressing in special garments prescribed for the ceremony, the High Priest proceeded as follows:

1. The bullock was slaughtered and the blood collected.

2. The Most Holy Place was entered for the first time and a cloud of incense created inside, to protect the priest from the splendor of the Lord during the ceremony.

3. The Most Holy Place was entered for the second time and some of the bull's blood was sprinkled on the Atonement Cover of the Ark of the Testimony and into the room, to

make atonement for his sins and those of his household.

4. The goat was slaughtered and the blood collected.

5. The Most Holy Place was entered for the third time and some of this blood was again sprinkled on the Atonement Cover of the Ark of the Testimony and into the room, this time to make atonement for the sins of his people.

6. The bull's blood and goat's blood were sprinkled around the Holy Place.

7. The bloods were mixed and sprinkled on the Altar of Burnt Offering to cleanse it.

8. The sins of the people were confessed over the scapegoat and it was led into the wilderness.

9. One ram was sacrificed as a burnt offering to make atonement for the High Priest.

10. The other ram was sacrificed as a burnt offering to make atonement for the people.

The ceremony ended with the High Priest burning the remains of the sin offerings and washing himself and his garments.

While studying the Day of Atonement, I came upon an interesting fact. The Most Holy Place within the Tabernacle was a perfect cube, thought to be 9 or 10 cubits on a side. I also noted that the Most Holy Place within the later Solomon's Temple was cubic, this time 20 cubits on a side. The New Jerusalem, another type of Most Holy Place, will be a cube 12,000 stadia (1382 miles) on a side (Revelation 21.16). In other words, *in the Bible the Most Holy Place was always a perfect cube*. This immediately sparked my interest, because I had found a nest of cubes encoded within the names of the 9/11 targets. I read more about the Crucifixion and the Day of Atonement with a mounting sense that I was myself crossing an important threshold.

In Matthew, Mark and Luke we are told of a signal event that happened at the moment of Jesus' death on the Cross: 'The curtain of the temple was torn in two from top to bottom' (Mark 15.38, NIV). This verse was telling us that the barrier previously in place between God and his people had been shattered by God himself (which was why it was torn from the top down). In other words, God was no longer confined to the Most Holy Place within the Tabernacle, but was now freely available to all who sought him through Jesus Christ. This is why Christians see no further need for a Day of Atonement.

Since 9/11 appeared to have symbolized the Crucifixion, could it also have symbolized the event the Crucifixion superseded: the Day of Atonement? The encoded cubes certainly hinted at a link with the Day of Atonement, as did the three successful air attacks on 9/11, which, I realized, could have symbolized the three times the High Priest entered the Most Holy Place and/or the crossing of the three thresholds by the High Priest as he entered the Most Holy Place. The slicing into each building of the hijacked airplanes was also symbolic of the tearing of the temple curtain as Jesus died on the Cross.

In the time of Jesus the Day of Atonement sacrifices took place in the Jerusalem temple, so I looked at diagrams of the temple to see how my hypothesis would work in this setting. There were two versions of the temple, both with the same essential structure as the Tabernacle, although differing in many details. The first temple was built by King Solomon, but later destroyed. A second temple was built in the time of Ezra and Nehemiah and this was later extended by Herod (figure 11)

Figure 11 The Second Temple

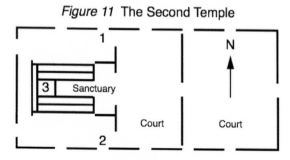

The layout was more complex than that of the Tabernacle. Instead of one entrance to the outer court there were now a large number of gates, possibly thirteen (the precise layout is not known). These had several different functions, but only two are identified here, for clarity: the two gates of offering. The sacrifice gate (1) was situated on the north side of the temple precinct and was the only gate used for entering with Day of Atonement offerings. The firstborn gate (2) on the south side was used for entering with offerings of firstborn animals. The only other feature I have marked is the Most Holy Place (3), which was protected by a double curtain, the curtain that was torn at the moment Jesus died.

The relative locations of the two marked gates reminded me of the relative locations of the north and south towers. I looked up a plan of the World Trade Center Plaza as it was then and confirmed that the towers were aligned in a north–south direction. The sacrifice gates were entered from the north and south, so next I looked at the direction from which each plane had struck their target. Sure enough, the North Tower and South Tower had been struck (entered) from the north and the south, just as the two sacrifice gates would have been entered from these directions (figure 12).

Figure 12 The Attacks on the Twin Towers

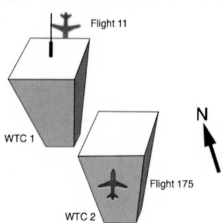

There was a clear parallel to be drawn here. The attack on the North Tower (WTC 1) by Flight 11 symbolized entrance to the temple via the sacrifice gate. The destruction of the South Tower (WTC 2) by Flight 175 symbolized entrance to the temple via the firstborn gate (this would also then point to the sacrifice of Jesus Christ, the 'firstborn son', on the Cross). The attack on the Pentagon by Flight 77 would then have to represent the entrance by the High Priest into the Most Holy Place. So whether it was viewed in terms of the Tabernacle or the Jerusalem Temple, I was by now fairly sure that a third function of 9/11 was to *symbolize the Day of Atonement.*

I thought back to the dream that has haunted me all my life and with which I opened this book. Chased by a witch, I ran through two doors, the second of which had an apple for a handle. In addition to what I've already written, there was one more interpretation I could now make. In the dream, I represented the High Priest. The first door symbolized the door to the outer court of the Tabernacle and the second door symbolized the entrance to the tent. The apple handle stood for the Most Holy Place through the Pentagon, because the apple is botanically related to the five-petaled rose and has a pentagonal arrangement of pips, and the Pentagon encodes both the number five (apple) and the cube (Most Holy Place).

I had accounted for the parts played by flights 11, 175 and 77 in the 9/11 drama. However, there was also Flight 93, which crashed in Pennsylvania: that couldn't be ignored. Then there was the mysterious collapse of WTC 7, which no hijacked airplane had hit. I felt that if 9/11 really had been an enactment of the Day of Atonement, then these two events should be explainable within that context.

The twin towers had always reminded me of a pair of horns and so I turned to the sacrifices of the five animals, all horned, that the ceremony required and which I had also so far ignored. The disposal of each animal is summarized below, given in the order in which the events took place:

1. A bullock was sacrificed as a sin offering for the High Priest and its blood sprinkled in the Most Holy Place.
2. A young goat was sacrificed as a sin offering for the people and its blood also sprinkled in the Most Holy Place.
3. The scapegoat had the sins of the people laid upon it then was led into the wilderness.
4. A ram was burnt as an offering for the High Priest.
5. Another ram was burnt as an offering for the people.

Five major events, involving four hijacked flights, took place on 9/11 and I eventually saw that they were equivalent to each of the Day of Atonement sacrifices, occurring in the same chronological order.

1. Flight 11 struck the North Tower (WTC 1) at 8:46 a.m. This was equivalent to the sacrifice of the bullock.
2. Flight 175 struck the South Tower (WTC 1) at 9:03 a.m. This was equivalent to the sacrifice of the goat.
3. Flight 93 was hijacked about 9:28 a.m., then began to veer off-course at 9:35 a.m. This was equivalent to the scapegoat being led out into the wilderness. After passengers bravely took on the hijackers, it crashed in the 'wilderness' of Somerset County, Pennsylvania, at 10:03 a.m.
4. Flight 77 struck the Pentagon at 9:37 a.m. This was equivalent to the sacrifice of the first ram for the High Priest.
5. WTC 7 collapsed at 5:20 p.m. after extensive damage from fires and falling debris. This was equivalent to the sacrifice of the second ram for the people.

There were many other parallels between the Day of Atonement rituals and 9/11. For example, the smoke rising from the towers represented the clouds of incense, and the sprinkling of the blood of the sacrificed animals was reenacted in the deaths of the victims.

Encodings within the NIV Bible only confirmed the connection between 11 September and the Day of Atonement. For example, two chapters in Exodus described the Lord's instructions for building, and the actual building of, the Altar of Burnt Offering. These are Exodus 27 and 38, which, I found, were the Bible's 77th and 88th chapters. These numbers, apart from being multiples of 11 (suggesting a link to 9/11), are the ordinal values of 'Christ' (77) and 'Immanuel' (88), again linking 9/11, the Crucifixion and the Day of Atonement.

Another likely allegory of 9/11 was an odd passage inserted into Leviticus, between chapters describing rules and laws for worship, sacrifice and the priesthood. This was the account of Aaron's two sons, Nadab and Abihu, who were killed by the Lord for offering unauthorized fire before him, and it was presumably inserted there to illustrate the importance of following God's ordinances. The verse describing their deaths is Leviticus 10.2: 'So fire came out from the presence of the LORD and consumed them, and they died before the LORD.' The ordinal value of the verse is 814 (11 x 74). It appeared to me, therefore, that the killing of Aaron's two sons for their profanity was a parable of the fall of the twin towers, also 'killed' for their profanity.

* * *

By now I thought I had fully understood this part of the September-11 Code. I was soon to come unstuck, however. When I looked at the attack on the Pentagon, I found a niggling difference between the atonement rite and 9/11. In both tabernacle and temple the High Priest entered the Most Holy Place from the *east*, passing through the curtain with the burning coals and sacrifices. However, the Pentagon was struck on its *west* side. This was the sort of little flaw that ripped huge holes in carefully spun theories, so I put the theory to one side for the moment. If this really was a divine message it had to be internally consistent.

Two internet acquaintances came to my rescue, however. These were researchers Kathryn LeCorre and Karen Gush, who contacted me in 2010. (Soon after this initial contact I had separate visions of each woman, each smiling at me, which hinted they were going to be important in some way; I was eventually able to confirm that these astrally beamed images were accurate from photographs I saw of them.) They expressed an interest in my work, shared some of their own findings and introduced me to the outstanding writings of E. E. Brooks.[15] In an essay entitled 'The Union of the Spirit and Soul'[16] Brooks convincingly demonstrates that the Tabernacle was actually a metaphor for the *female torso*. In Hebrew the sides of the outer court were called *katheph* (shoulders), the sides of the Holy Place were named *tsela* (ribs) and the west wall of the Most Holy Place was called *yarek* (thighs). These details were lost in English translations, so this parallel is largely unknown to Christians (figure 13).

Figure 13 The Tabernacle as a Female Torso

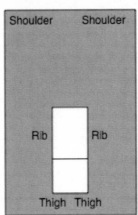

Brooks reasoned that if the western walls of the Most Holy Place are the thighs, then the Most Holy Place itself must be the womb. The entrance of the High Priest into the Most Holy Place on the Day of Atonement was then a metaphor for *the union of a male and a female.* Brooks showed how this interpretation made sense of the need for perfect animal sacrifices, the restriction on entering the Most Holy Place to the High Priest – who had to be a male – and the insistence on his ritual cleanliness and even on his physical perfection. This insistence on physical perfection extended to the High Priest's genitals. Brooks quoted Deuteronomy 23.1: 'No-one who has been emasculated by crushing or cutting may enter the assembly of the LORD.' To take part in this symbolic union the High Priest had to be a fully functioning male.

If the writings of E. E. Brooks and my own efforts had any value then they should harmonize, so I looked for connections to 9/11 in his work. I noticed that the chapter and verse indicators in Deuteronomy 23.1, quoted above, made 231 (11 x 21). Counting to Deuteronomy 23 from the Bible's beginning, I then discovered that this was the 176th chapter (11 x 16). These certainly did indicate a link to 9/11, and this link had to be through the items within the Ark of the Testimony, because, as Brooks showed, these signified the male's 'generative parts', with which Deuteronomy 23.1 was concerned: Aaron's rod that budded symbolized the penis, the pot of manna was sperm and the two tablets of the testimony were the testicles. The dream I recounted in chapter 3, which ended with two dogs jumping at me to bite my testicles, now made perfect sense. They were representing the twin towers, which had been 'crushed' on 9/11, signifying that the system they had stood for was 'not fit to enter the assembly of the LORD'.

In Brooks' essay I finally found a convincing explanation for the seeming inconsistency between the entrance of the High Priest into the Most Holy Place and the attack on the Pentagon.

Brooks stated that, since the Tabernacle symbolizes the female body and the western wall of the Most Holy Place represents the thighs, the correct entry point into the Most Holy Place for the High Priest, who represented the male, was not through the curtain on the east side but through the western wall. This was exactly what happened on 9/11, when the Pentagon was pierced on its west side (figure 14).

Figure 14 The Attack on the Pentagon

It all fitted perfectly now. Even the number of the flight that was hijacked and driven into the Pentagon, 77, was the ordinal value of 'Christ'. Bearing in mind the cubic shape of the Most Holy Place, which Brooks compares to the female womb, the statistics concerning those killed in the attack were also a fit. The number of Pentagon employees killed was 125, the cube of 5 again, and the number of passengers and crew killed was 64, the cube of 4.

One other point came from my reading of Brooks. If the Most Holy Place was a womb, it was reasonable to infer that the Ark of the Testimony was an egg. Since the Ark contained items that suggested a male, then the fertilization of the egg by the High Priest was designed to create a *male child*.

As I was writing this chapter I made a spectacular last-minute find that offered further support for these findings. I discovered that the ordinal values of the first twenty-four and thirty-seven words of the NIV Bible were the standard values of the following phrases, taken straight from the NIV Bible (they are generally called by different names in other versions).

First 24 words of NIV Bible (o) = 1169
Atonement Cover (s) = 1169

First 37 words of NIV Bible (o) = 1754
Ark of the Testimony (s) = 1754

The first twenty-four words also held the Signatures of Christ, as I showed in chapter 5; two of these are shown here along with the encodings related to the Ark of the Testimony (table 7.1).

Table 7.1 Jesus and The Ark in Genesis 1:1-2 (NIV)		
In the beginning God created the heavens and the earth. Now the (12 words)	earth was formless and empty, darkness was over the surface of the (12 words)	deep and the spirit of God was hovering over the earth. And God (13 words)
Jesus	Word	
Atonement Cover		
Ark of the Testimony		

The symbolism here was particularly appealing. Within the Ark of the Testimony and under the Atonement Cover were the most sacred objects in Judaism: the tablets, Aaron's rod that budded and the pot of manna. Within the encoding 'Ark of the Testimony' and coincident with the encoding 'Atonement Cover' were the six numerical signatures of Jesus Christ (chapter 5), whose name is held sacred by Christians. If the tablets *et al* represented the male generative parts then again the symbolism was perfect, as Jesus was a male. So the Ark of the Testimony was here being equated to Jesus Christ and its fertilization represented his coming into the world.

Brooks insisted that the sexual union of male and female symbolized by the Day of Atonement was in this context a metaphor for something purely spiritual. This was the seeding of God's Word in the minds of those who were prepared for it. Within the fertilized womb of that mind would then grow something Brooks called the 'manchild' (called the 'male child' in the NIV). This event was prophesied in Revelation 12.5. 'She gave birth to a son, a male child, who will rule all the nations with an iron sceptre. And her child was snatched up to God and to his throne.' Reading Brooks' essay, I realized, from my visions of the 'wise child', that this was exactly what had happened to me. Moreover, this being had revealed itself as no less than the Messiah: the wise child, the manchild and the Messiah were one and the same. Interestingly, the number encoded in the words spoken to me by the child, 358, was the standard value of both the Hebrew *Moshiach* (Messiah) and the English 'the manchild'. 'The male child' (NIV) was 343, the cube of 7 (the cube represents the Most Holy Place and perfection and 7 represents spiritual perfection) and the ordinal value of the charge against Jesus in Matthew: 'THIS IS JESUS, THE KING OF THE JEWS', as I showed in chapter 4.

So these encodings within the first few words of the NIV Bible, Brooks' esoteric interpretation of the Day of Atonement, the symbolism encoded within 9/11 and my own visionary experiences were all pointing to the same prophesied event: *the birth of the manchild, which was symbolically conceived on 9/11.*

The manchild/Messiah is elegantly symbolized by the Star of David, formed by the union of upward- and downward-pointing triangles, standing for the fusion of Spirit and matter. Taken together, the numbers 37 and 24, representing 'Ark of the Testament' and 'Atonement Cover', are connected with these ideas both numerically and geometrically. First of all, the product of the numbers 37 and 24 is the standard value of the Greek word for Jesus: Ihsous.

Ihsous (s, Gr.) = 888 = 37 x 24

Secondly, these numbers define hexagram 37, which has an outline of 24 discs.

* * *

One day in meditation I heard the words 'You are the apple.' This phrase has the same ordinal value as 'New York City' (168). Given that the apple symbolized the Most Holy Place, which in turn symbolized a womb, I think it was confirmation of the idea that our minds are the womb God seeds to produce the manchild. Just as the High Priest entered the Most Holy Place, Flight 77 pierced the Pentagon, two further flights tore into the Big Apple and the legendary William Tell split the apple on his son's head, so our minds have to be penetrated by God's Word if we are to be saved: our 'apple' has to be split.

In chapter 4 I showed evidence that 9/11 symbolized the Crucifixion. But the event was itself a crucifixion of the ego, a wounding of the collective pride of those who identified with western materialism (a sign that many people really had been deeply shaken by these events was that places of worship across the world were filled again for a while afterwards). The impact was magnified by the fact that the terrorists had the barest minimum of resources and by the worldwide coverage of the catastrophe. It has repeatedly been stated that 9/11 was the first major event to be witnessed in real time by almost the entire world. And what was the event they witnessed? It was the mighty USA being castrated (or perhaps circumcised) in front of a global audience, by a few fanatics armed with penknives.

We Christians know well that before we will turn to God we often have to be humbled in some way, because our pride is the biggest obstacle to conversion. The defeat of our ego lessens its grip on our lives and allows the seeding of something finer within us. The trials of my own life, seen in this light, were a blessing in disguise, crucifying my ego mind until its defenses were breached and the Light was able to enter. It appeared to me, then, that 9/11 was a token of this first stage of psycho-spiritual transformation, that the transformation is now taking place on a scale never before seen and that the entire process is beautifully symbolized by the concept of the birth of the manchild.

Chapter 8

The September-11 Cube

Therefore keep watch, because you do not know on what day your Lord will come.
     Matthew 24.42

One of the most rewarding benefits of my spiritual awakening was my new awareness of the importance of dreams. Once I really became attuned to them I realized I had a nightly source of insight, comfort and health advice. I was shown hidden parts of myself, challenged to grow and warned of trouble ahead. I could be told off when I deserved it, but also inspired to act and introduced to new possibilities. I also had in my possession a kind of oracle that showed me the real significance of my actions in life.

In 2003 I was given this dream: *I am a kind of sniffer dog, searching through scrub bush for something. Ahead I see a mound of earth I know is a lion's den, which has an entrance shaped like a vagina. I head straight for it. Inside are ancient and valuable scrolls and other treasures, along with chunks of meat; this is a great prize of some kind. I gobble up both the parchments and the meat. Then the whole scene is repeated. The second time I spot a huge spider, hidden in the mound under some earth, which is there to guard the treasures. I am told that the spider will die, but I insist on killing it anyway, attacking it with gusto and ripping its insides out. There is a feeling of great accomplishment.* The vagina hinted at the idea of sexual union and conception – interestingly, long before I had heard of the work of E. E. Brooks. However, the principal theme here was mythologist Joseph Campbell's concept of the hero's journey. This is a myth found in all cultures, where a journey is undertaken and a prize of great value won, often in the face of danger, then brought home. This dream was showing me I had entered the 'lion's den' and won my prize.

The rerun of the dream was something I had observed several times before – for instance, the angel dream I recounted in chapter 2 – and it suggested the idea of doubling, repetition and the number two, which I found quite puzzling. It had been most prevalent in 2001, at the time of my calling to find the code. On 11/11/01 I had an encounter with the Holy Spirit. Two days after that I was healed of a longstanding emotional problem and made my first code discoveries. Two days after that I had twice heard the overture *The Force of Destiny*, my Alpha Course director had twice heard a voice referring to me and two verses had appeared on her bookmark. There were two of us involved as well. This had to mean something.

I worked furiously on the code, most nights staying up well after midnight and retiring to bed only when I could no longer keep my eyes open. It was great fun finding material, although it could equally be frustrating to waste weeks or even months following blind leads, then have to discard it all and start again from scratch. I felt like I was trying to solve a jigsaw puzzle with only the vaguest idea of what picture the assembled pieces made. Or I was making my way through an immense forest by following a barely visible track. I would often mistake a random configuration of plants or a rabbit track for the main path and would wander down it until I was hopelessly lost, before retracing my steps until I was again on familiar territory. The more I searched, though, the easier it became to distinguish genuine codes from the kind of random numerical patterns to be found in all texts. The key was indispensable here, as were the many hints and clues I received.

So far the code seemed to be saying that 9/11 was a kind of staged drama, representing the Crucifixion of Jesus Christ and the Day of Atonement. The code and 9/11 were together dispensing a new revelation regarding the meaning of the Day of

Atonement: it was a symbolic union between male (High Priest) and female (Tabernacle), seeding the 'manchild' (Messiah) within it. 9/11 thus signified the conception of the manchild and my own experiences suggested that this event was an inner transformation of some kind.

After conception comes birth and it occurred to me that this might be signaled by some event yet to come. For the moment, though, I had several notebooks filled with findings I had yet to comprehend, so I let the future take care of itself while I occupied myself with completing the vast and complex puzzle before me.

In chapter 5 I noted that the individual names of the twin towers had ordinal values that summed to 386.

The North Tower + The South Tower (o) = 386

This was the standard value of 'Yeshua', the shorter of the two Hebrew words commonly used for Jesus:

Yeshua (s, Heb.) = 386

At first I thought that this was just some ornamentation on the code's structure, another sign that the destruction symbolized the Crucifixion. But then I discovered that 386 also had an important geometric property. My findings about the significance of 9/11 had resulted from my discovery of two cubes encoded within the names of the two structures attacked on 9/11: cube 125 and cube 343. My new finding was that cube 343 can be surrounded by a hollow cube of 386 spheres to create the cube of 9, 729 (figure 15).

Figure 15 Cube 343 and Cube 729

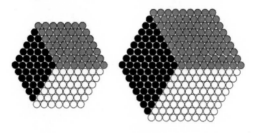

Nine was the biblical number of endings, finality, judgment, fruits and suffering, so the triple expression of that number had to be highly significant.

Piece after piece of this magnificent puzzle kept falling into place. I had now found three nested cubes encoded within the names of the structures attacked on 9/11.

The Pentagon (o) = 125 (cube of 5)

125 + The World Trade Center (o) = 343 (cube of 7)

343 + The North Tower + The South Tower (o) = 729 (cube of 9)

The discovery of a third encoded cube was a reassurance that this nest of cubes was a real phenomenon and no mere chimera. It was as deliberate as the attacks themselves. However, in contrast to those acts of destruction, these encoded numbers were the raw materials with which I was to build something. I already had part of the structure, of course, but this extra cubic layer suggested there was something more to find.

While studying the geometry of cubes, I discovered that when they are oriented in the way I have pictured, they project a hexagon. The 2-D projection of cube 729 was hexagon 217 (figure 16).

Figure 16 Cube 729 and Hexagon 217

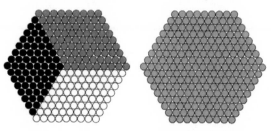

I recognised the number 217 from my study of 9/11 and the Bible. The three digits 2, 1 and 7 gave the numbers of the three WTC buildings that fell on 9/11 and also the order in which they did so:

1. WTC 2 fell at 09:59 a.m.
2. WTC 1 fell at 10:28 a.m.
3. WTC 7 fell at 05:20 p.m.

Even more mysteriously, the numbers 217 and 911 twice crossed each other within the Bible.

1. Genesis 9.11 was the Bible's 217th verse.
2. The Bible's 911th chapter was Haggai 2, which began, 'On the **twenty-first** day of the **seventh** month, the word of the LORD came through the prophet Haggai' (Haggai 2.1, emphasis added).

In Genesis 9.11, God tells Noah and his sons that he will establish his covenant with them. Could 9/11 have been signaling that a new covenant had been made? Haggai's two chapters concerned the rebuilding of the Jerusalem Temple, which I had already found connected with 9/11 (see chapter 6). All this fed my growing conviction that 9/11 was multisymbolic to an extraordinary degree and suggested that there was further gold to be mined from it.

Then one afternoon, as Karen and I relaxed in our lounge, I

found the biggest nugget of all. Karen was watching TV and I was sketching cubes (I'd been sketching geometric figures since I was a teenager, perhaps unconsciously preparing for this time). Suddenly, looking at the cube I'd just drawn, I saw something new: if three slices were cut through the centre of the cube in each spatial direction, a Star of David emerged (figure 17).

Figure 17 Three slices cut through a cube convey a Star of David

At that very moment Karen changed TV channels and I heard the opening lines of Cockney Rebel's 1975 hit 'Make Me Smile (Come Up and See Me)':[17]

You've done it all,
you've broken every code
and pulled the rebel to the floor.

I knew I had solved the final part of the puzzle. The nest of three cubes represented the Most Holy Place, or alternatively the Tabernacle/Temple, Holy Place and Most Holy Place. The three strikes on 9/11 represented the three incursions into the Most Holy Place by the High Priest during the Rite of Atonement; or, alternatively, the three thresholds the High Priest had to cross to reach the Most Holy Place from outside the Tabernacle; or in terms of the temple, the entrance through the sacrifice gates to north and south and the Most Holy Place itself. The High Priest entered the Most Holy Place from the east, but, in terms of the conception of the manchild he would now enter from the west, which would be a destructive act, as would be the tearing of the hymen or the crashing of an airplane into a building. I also knew that at the moment of Jesus' death on the Cross the curtain had been torn in two. Each strike could also then have symbolized the tearing of that curtain.

Bearing all this in mind, I made three symbolic slices through cube 729, by coloring the middle segment in each spatial direction. These represented the three entrances by the High Priest, the three thresholds to be crossed, the tearing of the curtain and the three airplane strikes on 9/11. The three strikes came from the north, south and west, so slicing through the cube in the three spatial directions (down, forward and right to left) was the nearest 3-D equivalent. The three slices created a figure I call *The September-11 Cube* (figure 18).

Figure 18 The September-11 Cube

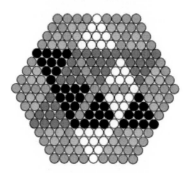

The September-11 Cube looked a bit like a Rubik's Cube, which was appropriate since both were puzzles. The solution to the puzzle posed by the September-11 Cube was found by orienting the cube as shown above and shining a light through the cube onto a flat surface (imagine that the spheres constituting the cube are made of glass and that the slices are colored). The projection on the surface is hexagon 217 with an internal Star of David (figure 19).

Figure 19 Hexagon 217 with Star of David

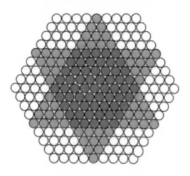

The Star of David has 121 discs, 121 being the ordinal value of these momentous words:

Second Coming (o) = 121

The Star also has an internal hexagon of 61 discs, which means that the six triangles forming the points of the star have 60 discs. These are the separate values of the two words:

Second (o) = 60
Coming (o) = 61

Since the total number of discs is 217, this means that there are 96 discs making up the six rhombi around the edge of the projected figure. 96 is the value of 'Christ's'. Therefore the entire projection of 217 discs delivers the same apocalyptic message:

Christ's Second Coming (o) = 217

Christ's (o) = 96 = discs in rhombi
Second (o) = 60 = discs in triangles
Coming (o) = 61 = discs in hexagon

Hidden within the September-11 Cube was the answer to my quest, the treasure waiting for me at the end of my journey, symbolized by this perfect marriage of word, number and form. The Star of David is the ideal object to symbolize Christ's return, as Jesus was a Jew from the line of David. This particular star is also perfect because of its natural and meaningful separation into the numbers 60 and 61, and also because 121 has a geometric link to the two numbers whose encoding within 9/11 began my quest, eleven and five. 121 is the *eleventh* square (11 x 11) and the *fifth* hexagram number.

Finally I understood why I'd had so many dreams and signs involving the number two: Christ was the *second* part of the Trinity and 9/11 marked *his Second Coming* (figure 20).

Figure 20 The Second Coming Symbolised
by Star of David 121

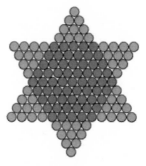

Second = 60 = discs in triangles
Coming = 61 = discs in hexagon

In answer to those who would claim that Jesus Christ could not have been the guiding hand behind 9/11, I quote some passages from the New Testament which plainly warned that our Lord's return was to be a day of calamity.

> At that time the sign of the Son of Man will appear in the sky, and all the nations of the earth will mourn. They will see the Son of Man coming on the clouds of the sky, with power and great glory.
> (Matthew 24.30)

Just as it was in the days of Noah, so also will it be in the days of the Son of Man. People were eating, drinking, marrying and being given in marriage up to the day Noah entered the ark. Then the flood came and destroyed them all.

(Luke 17.26–27)

... for you know very well that the day of the Lord will come like a thief in the night. While people are saying, 'Peace and safety', destruction will come on them suddenly, as labour pains on a pregnant woman, and they will not escape.

(1 Thessalonians 5.2–3)

But the day of the Lord will come like a thief. The heavens will disappear with a roar; the elements will be destroyed by fire, and the earth and everything in it will be laid bare.

(2 Peter 3.10)

I saw heaven standing open and there before me was a white horse, whose rider is called Faithful and True. With justice he judges and makes war.

(Revelation 19.11)

Even taking into account the hyperbole often found in Jewish and early Christian apocalyptic writing, there is no doubt that these passages were warning that Christ's return would be a day of destruction. We even sing about it in our songs and hymns:

Mine eyes have seen the glory of the coming of the Lord:
He is trampling out the vintage where the grapes of wrath are stored;
He hath loosed the fateful lightning of his terrible swift sword:
His truth is marching on.[18]

The NIV Bible itself was bookended with four confirmations that the Second Coming was upon us. In chapter 5, I showed the Signatures of Christ, which were encoded within the first twenty-four words of the NIV. The first two signatures were 'Jesus' and 'Yehoshua', encoded over the first eighteen words. However, 391 is also the standard value of 'Second Coming', so the first eighteen words simultaneously encrypt 'Jesus' and 'Second Coming' (table 8.1).

Table 8.1 First Eighteen Words Genesis (NIV)	
In the beginning God created the heavens and the earth. Now the (12 words)	earth was formless and empty, darkness (6 words)
Jesus	Second Coming

After I found this encoding I went to the other end of the NIV Bible and discovered that its last eighteen words were encoded too. These are '"… am coming soon." Amen. Come Lord Jesus. The grace of the Lord Jesus be with God's people. Amen' (Revelation 22.20–21), and they are encoded with 'The Lord' and 'Second Coming'. The encodings were organized in strings of nine words, which was also perfect because this was the very end of the Bible and nine is the number of endings, finality and judgment (table 8.2).

Table 8.2 Last Eighteen Words Revelation (NIV)	
"…am coming soon." Amen. Come Lord Jesus. The grace (9 words)	of the Lord Jesus be with God's people. Amen. (9 words)
The Lord	Second Coming

Next, I numerated the last few words of the Old Testament and the first few words of the New Testament and found that the last fourteen words of Malachi – '… their fathers; or else I will come and strike the land with a curse' (Malachi 4.6) – and the first fourteen words of Matthew – 'A record of the genealogy of Jesus

Christ the son of David, the son ...' (Matthew 1.1) – both had ordinal values of 604, which, miraculously, is the standard value of 'The Second Coming' (tables 8.3 and 8.4).

Table 8.3 Last Fourteen Words Malachi (NIV)
their fathers; or else I will come and strike the land with a curse. (14 words)
The Second Coming

Table 8.4 First Fourteen Words Matthew (NIV)
A record of the genealogy of Jesus Christ the son of David, the son (14 words)
The Second Coming

Why fourteen this time? If we read a little further on in Matthew, we see a reference to this number in the genealogy of Jesus, which is grouped into three lists of fourteen names: 'Thus there were fourteen generations in all from Abraham to David, fourteen from David to the exile in Babylon, and fourteen from the exile to the Christ' (Matthew 1.17). The Malachi encoding covers the fourteen words immediately before Matthew. The four encodings as a group bookend both testaments and give a neat 18-14-14-18 pattern.

* * *

So far, the Second Coming appeared to be manifesting principally within our western, Judeo-Christian culture. However I found indicators in other places. Some were the astronomical conjunctions I mentioned earlier: the total eclipse of 11 August, 1999, and the hexagonal planetary alignment on 11/9/03. Another portent, I thought, was the life of a white buffalo called Miracle, born in 1994 on a farm in Wisconsin.[19] The birth of this very rare white specimen was as significant to Native Americans as the Second Coming is to Christians. According to Sioux prophecy, the spirit of the White Buffalo Calf Woman would one day stand upon the earth as a white buffalo. Great changes would then happen. This buffalo would also go through a sequence of color changes – black, red and yellow – before returning to its white color. 9/11 occurred during Miracle's time on earth and she did in fact go through the color changes, which was remarkable enough. But what I found even more significant was that she lived for *exactly* 121 months (Miracle was born on 8/20/94 and died on 8/19/04) and that she survived a life-threatening operation when she was 61 months old. Incredibly, these numbers are the ordinal values of 'Coming', 'Miracle' (61) and 'Second Coming' (121). Her life span in days was 3652 (11 x 332).

I also received an incredible number of personal signs confirming that 9/11 really had signaled Christ's Second Coming. Many of these occurred before and around 2001, and I wrote about a few of them in earlier chapters. However, they persisted for years afterwards and in fact are still occurring as I write.

For instance, after returning from the carol service at my local church in the early hours of Christmas morning, 2004, I noticed that my car's odometer read 80808 (888 x 91). 888 is the standard value of 'The Lord's Second Coming' and 'Ihsous'.

In the summer of 2005, while I was waking up, I saw the words 'With You' appear three times in my field of vision. In the ordinal value system, With = 60 = Second, and You = 61 = Coming. The total of 121 multiplied by 3 gives 363, the standard value of *Ha Moshiach*, Hebrew for 'the Messiah'. So the vision was stating that the Messiah is with us and that this is the meaning of the Second Coming.

As if to firmly imprint in my mind the importance of my calling, significant markers in my own life and spiritual awakening had the ordinal values of 'Jesus Christ' (151) and 'Second Coming' (121) encoded within them. My birth date was 15,121 days before the end of the second millennium and I was given the key to the code on 15/11/2001. The birth dates of my wife and two daughters also contained significant numbers. My wife was born two years, two months and twenty days after me ('Second' (s) = 222), my eldest daughter was born 11,011 (121 x 91) days after me and my second and youngest daughter was born 11,511 days after me. My first grandson was also born a multiple of 121 days after me, and my second grandson was born in 2011 on the 11th day of the month.

The series of messages I received through synchronicities and angelic encounters, after reading *The Road Less Travelled* and watching *It's a Wonderful Life!* during the Christmas season of 1998, had also been timed to encode the gematria of the Second Coming. I revealed in chapter 1 that the third message occurred 666 days before the end of the second millennium. 666 is actually the standard value of one of the alternative phrases for the Second Coming:

The Lord's Coming (s) = 666

The starting point for these incredible experiences was Christmas Eve 1998, the day I borrowed *The Road* from my local library and also taped Frank Capra's film. This was 738 days before the end of the second millennium:

The Second Appearing (s) = 738

It was also 992 days before the events of 11 September, 2001:

The Appearing of Christ (s) = 992

In fact, these experiences were all exquisitely timed, but I would like to mention just one more: the second sign I received, after reading *Further along the Road Less Travelled*. This took place on 21 February, 1999, which was 679 days before the end of the second millennium:

Christ's Coming (s) = 679

A few years ago, I had a dream similar to the one with which I started this chapter: *I am at the end of my father's garden, digging the earth underneath his pigeon loft for something. A workmate with the initials S. C. is beside me doing the same. We each unearth a grail cup.* My father's garden was a reference to God's creation (like the dream in chapter 7). The pigeon loft at the end of the garden was a reference to our fallen world. The initials S. C. referred to the Second Coming, as did the fact that there were two of us and two grail cups. The grail cups themselves referred to the barely comprehensible fact that I had uncovered the alphanumerical Holy Grail.

Chapter 9

The Sign of the Cross

In nomine Patris et Filii et Spiritus Sancti. Amen.
The Sign of the Cross

In a whole series of dreams and visions I felt the approach of Jesus Christ. He appeared in various fascinating guises: as a fisherman (fisher of men), as a work colleague with the initials J. C., as a celebrity with the same initials, as two people with the initials J. E. and C. H. and in other ways. Although he appeared as many different characters, his eyes were always the same, shining with love and joy.

I was still working as a laboratory manager in a chemical factory, but I was hating every minute of it. The role into which I'd been thrust was alien to me, I hated the culture there and both my physical and mental health were suffering. I was also working hard on the code, which was taking up most of my energies. I knew I couldn't last much longer in a demanding and often frustrating job if I was to continue with what I now saw as my real work. I had changed inside too, and now had a longing to do something that increased the sum of human happiness, rather than fattening the company owner's wallet.

One lunchtime, while I was meditating, I had a vision of Jesus as the workmate I mentioned with the initials J. C. He walked up to me, beaming, and threw a teabag at me. In an earlier dream I had, I was working in the laboratory one bright day when a triangular spaceship made of blue spheres took me and flew me to Edinburgh, dropping me off in the district of Leith at night. Some time later I was made redundant from my job. I soon got another though, working nightshift for a Christian charity. The hostel was in Leith, Edinburgh, and was a converted tea factory – all hinted at in the dream and vision. I was much happier there and, more importantly, had more time and energy to devote to the code.

The evidence that the Second Coming of Jesus Christ really had arrived continued to accumulate. Yehoshua and Ihsous, the Hebrew and Greek words for Jesus, both have standard values of 391 and 888:

Yehoshua (s, Heb.) = 391
Ihsous (s, Gr.) = 888

These two numbers double as signifiers for the Second Coming:

Second Coming (s) = 391
The Lord's Second Coming (s) = 888

One day, looking through my old KJV Bible, I noticed an interesting sequence of numbers in the index of the books of the Bible. The index listed each book, along with the number of chapters in that book. Looking down the list I noticed that the numbers of chapters in three books near the end of the Old Testament – Joel, Amos and Obadiah – gave the digits 3, 9 and 1 in sequence (table 9.1)

Table 9.1 Books and Chapters in the Old Testament					
Book	Chap.	Book	Chap.	Book	Chap.
Genesis	50	2 Chron.	36	Daniel	12
Exodus	40	Ezra	10	Hosea	14
Leviticus	27	Nehemiah	13	**Joel**	**3**
Numbers	36	Esther	10	**Amos**	**9**
Deuter.	34	Job	42	**Obadiah**	**1**
Joshua	24	Psalms	150	Jonah	4
Judges	21	Proverbs	31	Micah	7
Ruth	4	Eccles.	12	Nahum	3
1 Samuel	31	S. of S.	8	Habakkuk	3
2 Samuel	24	Isaiah	66	Zephaniah	3
1 Kings	22	Jeremiah	52	Haggai	2
2 Kings	25	Lament.	5	Zechariah	14
1 Chron.	29	Ezekiel	48	Malachi	4

Knowing the significance of 391, I nosed around to see what else I could find. The first thing I noticed was that the standard value of the names of the three books was also 391.

Joel + Amos + Obadiah (s) = 391

Then I made what turned out to be, in a literal sense, a *crucial* find: Amos 9, the final chapter in the second of the three books, was the 888th chapter in the Bible (table 9.2)

Table 9.2 391 Crossing 888		
Book	Final Chapter	Place Value
Joel	3	879
Amos	**9**	**888**
Obadiah	1	889

The numbers 391 and 888 were therefore the stake and crossbar of a symbolic cross at Amos 9, symbolizing Jesus and his Second Coming, which I call the Sign of the Cross (figure 21).

Figure 21 The Sign of the Cross

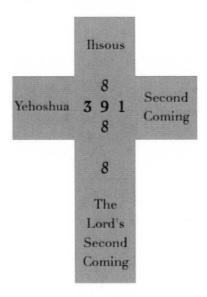

In addition to the significance of the cross in Christianity, crosses are used to mark the location of something important ('X marks the spot'). So naturally I wondered if there was any reason why this particular biblical location would be highlighted. Joel, Amos and Obadiah were three of the twelve so-called minor prophets, whose writings form the last twelve books of the Old Testament ('minor' refers not to their importance but to the brevity of their writings). A summary of the minor prophets, listed in biblical order along with the main themes they address in their writings, is given in table 9.3.[20]

Table 9.3 The Minor Prophets and their Themes	
Prophet	Main Themes of Book
Hosea	Salvation
Joel	**The Day of the Lord**
Amos	Judgment; **The Day of the Lord;** Redemption
Obadiah	The destruction of Edom; **The Day of the Lord**
Jonah	Serving the Lord; His mercy
Micah	Injustice; Oppression
Nahum	Judgment on Nineveh; comfort to Israel
Habakkuk	God embracing Judah; Chaldea's destruction
Zephaniah	God's anger; **The Day of the Lord;** Repentance
Haggai	The restoration of the Temple
Zechariah	Building the Temple; God's kingdom
Malachi	The messenger to come, **The Day of the Lord**

One theme stood out above all others: the Day of the Lord. Moreover, when I read Joel, Amos and Obadiah, the books forming the stake of the cross, I saw that the Day of the Lord was a major concern of each book. Of the other nine minor prophets, only Zephaniah and Malachi mention it. Of the five major books of prophecy (Isaiah, Jeremiah, Lamentations, Ezekiel and Daniel), only Isaiah and Ezekiel have the phrase 'Day of the Lord'. In fact, of the eighteen mentions of the phrase, fully nine are found just within Joel, Amos and Obadiah.

Knowing little about the Day of the Lord, I did some research, learning that it is a time when God's wrath is poured out on a people for their sins. It often referred to local judgments made on individual nations during biblical times. However, the Bible repeatedly insists that God will intervene in human affairs one last time, calling all nations to a final judgment. This ultimate 'Day of the Lord' will be one of terrible retribution. For example:

> The sun will be turned into darkness
> and the moon to blood
> before the coming of the great and dreadful day of the LORD.
> (Joel 2.31)

> Woe to you who long
> for the day of the LORD!
> Why do you long for the day of the LORD?
> That day will be darkness, not light.
> (Amos 5.18)

> 'Surely the day is coming; it will burn like a furnace. All the arrogant and every evildoer will be stubble, and that day that is coming will set them on fire,' says the LORD Almighty. 'Not a root or a branch will be left to them.'
> (Malachi 4.1)

My investigations had so far uncovered two numbers which happen to be the standard values of the Hebrew and Greek words for Jesus, and also of English phrases for the Second Coming, 'crossing' in the middle of a cluster of prophecies of the Day of the Lord. It was now time to take a look at the centerpoint of the cross, Amos 9, to see what hung there.

Amos is sometimes called 'the prophet of doom' and his book begins with God's condemnation both of Israel's neighbors and of Israel itself. The book nears its close with a series of five visions of God's judgment on Israel, and Amos 9.1–10 contains the last and most terrible of these: a picture of Israel's almost total destruction. The book also makes it clear that this punishment is inevitable. The cross, therefore, marks the exact site of one of the Bible's most significant end-time prophecies.

Here is how Amos 9 begins:

I saw the Lord standing by the altar, and he said:
'Strike the tops of the pillars
so that the thresholds shake.
Bring them down on the heads of all the people;
those who are left I will kill by the sword.
Not one will get away,
none will escape.'(Amos 9.1)

So that was it: another prophecy of 9/11! Flights 11 and 175 struck the twin towers near the tops of those 'pillars' and certainly brought them down on the heads of the people. I picked up my calculator and immediately found that the word 'cross' in English and its equivalent in Hebrew, *tav* (consisting of the letters Tav and Vav), were encoded over two consecutive nine-word strings (there again was nine, the number of endings, finality and judgment), starting from the beginning of Amos 9 (table 9.4).

Table 9.4 Two Encoded Crosses in Amos 9	
I saw the Lord standing by the altar, and (9 words)	*He said "Strike the tops of the pillars, so..."* (9 words)
o.v. = 353	o.v. = 406
Cross	Tav

The marking of this location with crosses was further support for my conclusion that 9/11 was a kind of crucifixion. Furthermore, the man who 'crucified' the World Trade Center and Pentagon was Osama bin Laden, the name 'Osama bin Laden' having the same standard value as 'cross'.

The words spoken by the Lord in this opening verse were also encrypted, this time over two strings of 19 words. The encoded numbers were 911, 888 and 391, which were a concise summary of the September-11 Code. 911 was self-explanatory and 888 and 391 were the two cross numbers (table 9.5).

Table 9.5 Encodings Within the Lord's Words in Amos 9.1		
Strike the tops of the pillars so that the thresholds shake. Bring them down on the heads of all (19 words)	the people; those who are left I will kill (9 words)	with the sword. Not one will get away, none will (10 words)
911	888	
	391	

I found more encodings here, but the evidence I've shown was enough to convince me that *the terrorist attacks on 11 September, 2001, were the prophesied Day of the Lord.* The physical destruction wrought on that day was tiny compared to the expectations of the Old Testament prophets and modern Christian literalists, but the impact on our collective psyche was cataclysmic. I thought back to the images the world saw on that shocking day. As the dust and smoke from the fallen towers blotted out Manhattan, 'the city that never sleeps' was for once stunned into an eerie quietude, completely overwhelmed by the magnitude of the disaster. Even from the safety of my living room it felt like a terrible day of reckoning to me (see photograph).

Other encodings in passages referring to the Day of the Lord only added to what I'd found. For instance, Zephaniah 1.16 prophesies that the 'great day of the Lord' will be

a day of trumpet and battle cry

against the fortified cities
and against the corner towers.

This verse has an ordinal value of 847 (11 x 11 x 7), confirming again that the Day of the Lord had finally come.

If the Bible's 888th chapter was crossed with 391, what about the 391st chapter? This was 2 Chronicles 24. Just as the code used 18 as shorthand for 666, so it looked as if 24 was being used as shorthand for 888, as it is 8 + 8 + 8. Also, the number 888 is the standard value of 'Ihsous' and 24 is the reduced value of the same word. So 391 and 888 were crossing again, in a manner of speaking. 2 Chronicles 24 tells how one of the kings of the Israelites, Joash, repaired the Jerusalem Temple. This echoes Amos 9.11, where the Lord tells Amos that he will repair the tent of David, a type of tabernacle. So both locations are associated with the repairing of the house of God, as, it seemed likely, was 9/11 itself.

Later, I found the numbers 391 and 888 encoded within the genealogy of Adam and his descendants in the book of Genesis. This listing, which runs through the book, gives the life span of each male from Adam to Joseph, and usually includes their age at the birth of their first son and either the number of years they lived after that or their total life span.

The line includes Noah, who survived the Flood by building an ark on the instructions of God; Abraham, the first of the three patriarchs, who led his people to the land of Canaan, again on God's orders; and Joseph, who was sent to Egypt to save his brothers and later called his family down from Canaan to save them from a famine. These three leaders created some of the definitive events in the Genesis narrative, leading their people through important transitional periods. In a sense all three were saviors of their people.

I noticed that most of the genealogical information was given in Genesis 5 and 11. Since 5 and 11 had been the two numbers encoded within the Pentagon and twin towers, it occurred to me that the list might be concealing something. So I tried adding the numbers in these chapters in different ways, finding tantalizing but incomplete glimpses of a code. Only when I discovered that the list actually extended beyond Genesis 11 to the end of the book was I able to put it all together.

The entire genealogical list from Adam to Joseph is tabulated below (table 9.6).

Table 9.6 The Genealogical List in Genesis							
Order	Location	Place Value	Name	A	B	C	Running Total
1	5:3-5	-	Adam	130	800	930	1860
2	5:6-8	-	Seth	105	807	912	3864
3	5:9-11	-	Enosh	90	815	905	5494
4	5:12-14	-	Kenan	70	840	910	7314
5	5:15-17	-	Mahalalel	65	830	895	9104
6	5:18-20	-	Jared	162	800	962	11028
7	5:51-23	-	Enoch	65	300	365	11758
8	5:25-27	-	Methus.	187	782	969	13696
9	5:28-31	-	Lamech	182	595	777	15250
10	5:32	-	Noah	500	-	-	15750
11	9:28-29	-	Noah	-	350	950	**17050**
12	11:10-11	-	Shem	100	500	-	17650
13	11:12-13	-	Arphaxad	35	403	-	18088
14	11:14-15	-	Shelah	30	403	-	18521
15	11:16-17	-	Eber	34	430	-	18985
16	11:18-19	-	Peleg	30	209	-	19224
17	11:20-21	-	Reu	32	207	-	19463
18	11:22-23	-	Serug	30	200	-	19693
19	11:24-25	-	Nahor	29	119	-	19841
20	11:26-32	-	Terah	70	-	205	20116
21	21:5	-	Abraham	100	-	-	20216
22	25:7	666	Abraham	-	-	175	**20391**
23	25:26	-	Isaac	60	-	-	20451
24	35:28	-	Isaac	-	-	180	20631
25	47:28	-	Jacob	-	-	147	20778
26	50:22	1529	Joseph	-	-	110	**20888**

Key: Each numbered row represents the biblical location of a number concerning the life span of one of that line. The chapter and verse where it is found is given in the second column on the left. The third column on the left shows the place value of selected verses – only those of interest are shown. The next column gives the names of each male in the generational line, the three columns after it (A, B and C), showing the details of their life spans; note that these columns are based on the biblical layout. The right-hand column shows the running totals of all the numbers in the three columns.

This list had been sitting within Scripture for thousands of years, yet, incredibly, it whispered to me of recent events. Countless biblical scholars, kabbalists and would-be code breakers would have pored over these numbers before me, but for them the figures would have been silent, because the Second Coming had to come to pass before the numbers could speak. Nor did others have the knowledge I possessed, drummed into me by angelic tutors, by the key to the code and by my growing expertise in uncovering the September-11 Code. Three things leaped out at me right away.

Firstly, the eleventh sum, to Noah, was 17,050, or 11 x 1550. This was the only one of the subtotals to be a multiple of eleven. The chapter here was 9 and it was the only subtotal associated with this chapter; this confluence of elevens in chapter 9 indicated that this list might be connected to 9/11 in some way.

Secondly, the sum to the 666th verse was 20,391, the final three digits of which are 391, the standard value of 'Second Coming' and 'Yehoshua'. The number 666, I now knew, was the value of 'The Lord's Coming'. In keeping with the eleven pattern, this was row 22, and the summed ordinal values of the first twenty-two names on these lists was 1111 (11 x 101). Yet again the code was linking 11 (9/11) with the beast and the Second Coming (666 and 391).

Thirdly, the sum to the 1529th verse was 20,888. So the 'cross' numbers 391 and 888 were both found in this table, albeit as the last three digits of larger numbers. The number two, in this context, had to be a reference to the Second Coming. The zero was being used as a spacer, separating the other digits into two meaningful parts.

What about 1529? Confluences of meaningfully related numbers were the backbone of the code and if 1529 meant nothing then this would all collapse into a heap of random numbers. However, 1529 (which was also a multiple of 11) happened to be the standard value of these words:

Jesus Christ + The Second Coming (s) = 1529
The return of Jesus (s) = 1529

There was one more significant number encoded here. 20,888, the number ending the list, is 373 x 56, 373 being the standard value of the Greek Logos, which means 'Word'.

Logos (s, Gr.) = 373

Finally, the three encoded numbers were associated with the three figures who were saviors to their people: Noah, who saved them from the Flood; Abraham, who led his people to Canaan; and Joseph, who saved his family from a famine. All three men were types of savior (and thus forerunners of Christ) and all three episodes in the history of the Israelites were being used as parables of the Second Coming.

* * *

I also found several further meaningful alignments of chapter place value and narrative in the Bible. For example, the Bible's 925th chapter is Zechariah 14, subtitled (in the NIV) *The LORD Comes and Reigns* and beginning, 'A day of the LORD is coming when your plunder will be divided among you' (Zechariah 14.1). This was therefore another reference to the Day of the Lord, and, for Christians, the Second Coming, because the number 925 is the standard value of this name:

Jesus Christ (s) = 925

Another example was the Bible's 1185th chapter, which is Revelation 18. This has one theme throughout: the fall of Babylon the Great.

With a mighty voice he shouted:
'Fallen! Fallen is Babylon the Great!
She has become a home for demons
and a haunt for every evil spirit,
a haunt for every unclean and detestable bird.'
(Revelation 18.2)

Eighteen is used as shorthand for 666 in the code, hinting at a link with 9/11, a link that is strengthened by the place value of the chapter:

The Second Coming of Jesus (s) = 1185

So 9/11, which was the signal event for the Second Coming, also appeared to be *the fall of Babylon the Great*.

Woe! Woe, O great city,
O Babylon, city of power!
In one hour your doom has come!
(Revelation 18.10)

* * *

There's a poignant sense of aloneness that comes with the discovery of something new. You become separated from the flow of everyday life, carried off by powerful currents to a place from which you can never return. Already an introvert, I slowly became something of a recluse, giving up my hobby of amateur music and spending almost all of my spare time working on the code, my burden but also my great joy. However, I knew that the arcane knowledge I'd stumbled upon could not be for me alone, so I began to give talks and radio interviews on the code (which I surprised myself by enjoying) created a website, wrote articles, answered emails and made a first attempt at a book. All this kept me occupied and partly allayed my feelings of isolation. Maybe I could never leave my new abode, but I could call others to it.

I also told selected friends, work colleagues, family members and fellow Christians about my work. But this tactic backfired on me for the most part, as people projected their own beliefs, fears and prejudices onto both the code and myself, or worse, were apathetic about it all. This seemed like a fulfillment of the prophetic dream I had in 2000, in which, as Mr. Spock, I was attacked and rejected for telling others something important.

Perhaps not surprisingly, the Christian community in the small town in which I lived seemed the most suspicious of me and the least interested in learning something new. It quickly became obvious that I was not going to be welcome in any local church if I continued to blab to them about my code work or even my spiritual experiences. Most Christians are wary of the unorthodox and suspicious of anything that smacks of the occult (a word that simply means 'hidden' but which now carries around all kinds of heavy baggage). I flitted around from church to church but never really found one that I felt comfortable with.

After a few years as a Christian I came to the sad realization that no church would accept me as a member unless I played ignorant and kept my esoteric knowledge from the exoteric majority. But this is something of which I am incapable of doing for any length of time and anyway feel is a denial of my vocation. I became so distressed by my dilemma that by 2008 I was on the brink of giving up the practice of Christianity and going it alone. However, something held me back from doing it.

Standing on the outskirts of the Christian flock has given me a clearer view than I would have gotten near the centre, but it is also a riskier place to be, because the sheep on the edge of the flock are more likely to be picked off by wolves. I gradually came under intense spiritual attack, probably peaking around 2008 or 2009, a period during which I was making great strides in my understanding of the code, but floundering as a Christian.

The spiritual battle I found myself engaged in reached its denouement in December 2009. I woke up one morning sensing with my inner vision that I was within a vast, though enclosed, space (yet simultaneously aware of lying in bed). I felt a low, almost sexual, thrill alongside a sense of oppression and restriction. One entire wall of this humongous vault was a mirror and I could see a pair of sinister, neon-blue eyes behind it, silently watching me, waiting for something. I knew all I had to do was yield and I would be allied with, or perhaps belong to, the owner of those eyes. Instinctively, I began to recite the name 'Jesus Christ' over and over again in my head. However, every time I tried to produce the name it came out garbled. Sensing real danger now, I persevered and eventually the name came out correctly, at which point the nightmarish vision ended. That morning I fully appreciated the power of the Lord's name in dispelling unwanted attention. I also decided it might be better to stay within the fellowship of the Church to the extent that I was able. It might be dangerous to situate yourself on the outskirts of the flock, but it was positively suicidal to go wandering off into the wilderness alone.

During this period I learned in a vivid dream that the primary mode of attack on the Church is through perversion of the sex instinct: *I am shown scenes of people indulging in various sexual perversions. Then I am taken to a room where two witches are conferring. They are unaware that I am present and I overhear one telling the other that "Christianity is to be defeated through sexual immorality." Then I am shown a scene where a huge witch's head tries to force its way into a house, which I know represents myself. The door just holds firm and the witch retreats.* This last dream scene seemed to indicate that the barrage of spiritual attacks I had been facing would abate, which they eventually did, to some extent.

There was more trouble on the material plane too. My initial naivety with regard to what was acceptable thought and practice in Christian circles led, surreally, to suspicions at the Christian charity where I now worked that I was a Satanist (I knew then that my chances of ever being promoted were slim, guessing there might be a glass ceiling for Satanists in a Christian organisation). So I learned - all-too-slowly, mind you - what I could say and who I could say it to and quietly got on with my code work, accepting the difficulties and challenges it brought and praying regularly to the God who had so graciously allowed me to serve both him and my fellow man in such an exciting and fulfilling way.

Chapter 10

The Creation Snowflake

Nature is full of genius, full of the divinity; so that not a snow-flake escapes its fashioning hand.
Henry David Thoreau

As I write these words it looks certain to be a white Christmas this year, which delights me because I have always been enchanted by snow. A fresh snowfall is one of nature's miracles, brightening the drabbest landscape, adding excitement to the dullest day and forcing all of us, even those who try to shut nature out of their lives with all the technological blinkers of civilization, to acknowledge its transforming power and timeless beauty.

Snow is even more beautiful under a microscope, as I once discovered when I was a boy. As soon as I peered through the lens I entered a realm of pristine beauty and infinite variety. I soon noticed, however, that it was a world with one unifying feature: each snow crystal had six branches (figure 22).

Figure 22 Snow Crystal

In fact, beneath the complexity of snow crystals is a very simple object: the hexagon. I was already familiar with hexagon 7 in my early forays into the world of figurate numbers, and this object could be thought of as a simple snow crystal (figure 23).

Figure 23 **Hexagon 7**

Genesis tells us that seven is the number of days God took to create heaven and earth. The last day, however, was one of rest, so the Creation week was split into six working days and a day of rest. As I researched this topic I read in Leonora Leet's *The Secret Doctrine of the Kabbalah* that in Judaism the seven days of Creation are sometimes visualized as hexagon 7. This is because the six outer discs can represent the six creation days.

This ring surrounds a space into which a seventh disc can be put, symbolizing the day of rest (figure 24).

Figure 24 **The Creation Week as a Hexagon**

In nature, larger structures are built from smaller units. So atoms come together to form molecules, which bond to create snow crystals, which accumulate into snowflakes, these falling from the sky to create a blanket of snow. Thinking about this, I wondered what would happen if I used the product of the first Creation week, hexagon 7, as the day unit for a second illustration of the Creation week. What I created, to my surprise, was a numerical snowflake, made from 55 individual discs (figure 25).

Figure 25 Snowflake 55

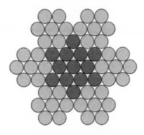

This time the free space was unexpectedly filled with a hexagram, or Star of David. This seemed very apt for the seventh day, which was God's day of rest and the first holy day.

As with triangles, there is an infinite series of hexagons. The next figure in the hexagon series is hexagon 19 (figure 26).

Figure 26 Hexagon 19

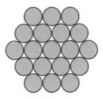

Using this figure I built a third model of the Creation week, which produced a beautiful snowflake, fashioned from 151 individual discs (figure 27).

Figure 27 Snowflake 151

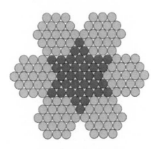

I suspected that snowflake 151 was much more than a mere Christmas decoration, though, because 151 was a familiar number to me: it was the ordinal value of 'Jesus Christ' and 'Holy Spirit'. Was that just coincidence? I would have to investigate further to be sure. What I found after doing so was that the seventh-day hexagram of 37 discs (which could also be thought of as the seed from which the snow crystal grew) was also connected to the Trinity through the reduced values of these names:

Spirit (r) = 37
The Lord (r) = 37

My next thought was to use snowflake 151 as the unit for the six-day ring. This resulted in a glittering snowflake made from 1279 individual discs I call the *Creation Snowflake* (figure 28).

Figure 28 The Creation Snowflake

The Creation Snowflake has an outer ring of 906 (6 x 151) discs, representing the six working days of creation, surrounding a beautiful snowflake of 373 discs, this symbolizing the seventh day. It's worth taking a look at snowflake 373 on its own (figure 29).

Figure 29 Snowflake 373

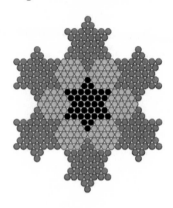

Snowflake 373 has some of the complexity of real snow crystals and is a particularly lovely figure. I couldn't see a connection to the Trinity, however, so I put this part of the project aside for the moment. Then I came across the Biblewheel website run by Richard McGough.[21] Independently of me, he had discovered snowflake 373, but to my delight I read that he had also found that 373 is the standard value of the Greek word *Logos*, meaning 'Word'. When Jesus of Nazareth was born 'the Word became flesh' (John 1.14), so it seemed more than coincidence that snowflake 373 contained snowflake 151, representing 'Jesus Christ' and 'Holy Spirit', and hexagram 37, depicting 'the Lord' and 'Spirit'. I looked again at the Creation Snowflake, and further connections came as thick and fast as snowflakes from a leaden sky.

The number of discs in snowflake 1279 is actually the sum of the values of the Greek and Hebrew words for Jesus:

Ihsous (s, Gr.) = 888
Yehoshua (s, Heb.) = 391
888 + 391 = 1279

The number of discs in the outer ring, 906, is the sum of the English and Hebrew words for Jesus:

Jesus (s) = 515
Yehoshua (s, Heb.) = 391
515 + 391 = 906

That was sensational. What was more, I already knew that the number 906 was the ordinal value of the first eighteen words of the NIV Bible:

In the beginning God created the heavens and the earth. Now the earth was formless and empty, darkness (o) = 906

I looked at other properties of the snowflake. The number of discs around its periphery was 252. I knew this number too. It was the ordinal value of the first six words of Genesis.

In the beginning God created the (o) = 252

Could the entire figure be encoded within the first few words of the NIV Bible? It seemed too much to hope for, because I'd already found an incredible amount of information at that very location. For these to be genuine encodings, though, I would have to find the number that represented the complete snowflake: 1279. In fact it is the ordinal value of the second verse of the NIV Bible:

Now the earth was formless and empty, darkness was over the surface of the deep, and the Spirit of God was hovering over the waters. (o) = 1279

So three numbers, representing the Creation Snowflake and its two major structural properties, were encoded within the first two verses of the NIV Bible. The structure these numbers highlighted was the one that emerges from the Creation week model I used to grow the snowflake. Therefore both snowflake and construction method were neatly encoded (table 10.1)

Table 10.1 The Creation Snowflake in Genesis 1.1-2 (NIV)			
In the beginning God created the	heavens and the earth.	Now the earth was formless and empty, darkness	was over the surface of the deep and the spirit of God was hovering over the waters.
Outline			
Outer Ring			
		Complete Snowflake	

I liked the way the encoding of the snowflake implied a gradual crystallization or manifestation: first there was the outline, then the rest of the outer ring, then the entire crystal. What interested me even more, though, was the fact that two of these three numbers were part of the same pattern of sixes that revealed the Signatures of Christ. Moreover, the Creation Snowflake is a six-sided figure, so it had to be deliberate planning that these numbers were encoded along with the six signatures of Christ, in six-word strings, within a passage summarizing the six working days of Creation.

It's a good idea to put things down in visual form – tables, flow charts, diagrams, etc – because pearls that would otherwise be hidden can suddenly glisten in the new light you've shone on them. When I created the table above, I suddenly saw a number that had up till then remained unnoticed. Words 11 to 18, which lie between the start of Genesis 1.2 and the end of the outer ring encoding, have an ordinal value of 476. This is the standard value (as usual) of the following title:

The Messiah (s) = 476

These Creation snowflake encodings perfectly mesh with the Signatures of Christ, revealing a larger pattern and showing that the same divine artist created both (table 10.2).

Table 10.2 Creation Snowflake and Signatures of Christ				
Outline	Messiah	Yehoshua	Messiah	
	Word			
Outer Ring				
		The Messiah		
		Complete Snowflake		
Jesus		Word		

A flurry of signs swirled around my discovery of the Creation Snowflake. For instance, the day I did a page on the snowflake and put it on my website turned out to be 1279 days since 9/11. I was beyond astonishment by this stage.

I discovered that the Creation Snowflake is related to a mathematical object known as the Koch snowflake. The Koch snowflake was discovered about a century ago but was regarded as a mathematical curiosity. It was only in 1977 that mathematician Benoit Mandelbrot published *Fractals: Form, Chance and Dimension*, showing that objects like the Koch snowflake, known as fractals, are in fact approximated in nature. The geometry of the universe is fractal geometry. What then were the chances that the Creation Snowflake should just happen to be found within the verses describing God's creation of heaven and earth? The odds just kept piling up. The first edition of the NIV Bible was published in 1973, so these words were already written and encoded long before even mathematicians, far less Bible scholars, knew about our fractal universe.

Interestingly, the outline of the snowflake is also found in the KJV Bible, because the NIV shares its first six words with the KJV Bible, which was published in 1611: 'In the beginning God created the ...' The Creation Snowflake had taken centuries to crystallize. There is a movement among some conservative Christians to denigrate the NIV and other modern versions of the Bible, because of small changes in the text from the KJV Bible. But for me the September-11 Code is evidence that God himself is not only perfectly okay with the NIV Bible, but that he had begun to create the biblical part of the code long before the NIV existed. I thought that this might be all the Creation Snowflake had to say to us, but I had still to hear the greatest message of all. I had already found that the number 1279 was the sum of 391 and 888, giving 'Yehoshua' and 'Ihsous'. However, these numbers are also the standard values of 'Second Coming' and 'The Lord's Second Coming', so I could also pair the phrases this way:

Ihsous + Second Coming (s) = 1279
Yehoshua + The Lord's Second Coming (s) = 1279

I began to search for more pairings. There are other terms for the Second Coming, particularly 'Second Advent' and 'Second Appearing'. I numbered these phrases and reached for my trusty calculator. This, believe it or not, is what I found:

The Lord + Second Advent (s) = 1279
Yehoshua HaMoshiach + Second Appearing (s) = 1279

'Yehoshua HaMoshiach' (spelled Yod He Shin Vav Ayin, He Mem Shin Yod Chet) is the Hebrew name and title meaning 'Jesus the Messiah'. Finally, I tried another phrase occasionally used, 'Second Manifestation', and found that it paired with a Hebrew word sometimes used for Jesus: YHShVH (Yod He Shin Vav He), which is the personal name of God, YHVH, with the addition of a Shin:

YHShVH + Second Manifestation (s) = 1279

Finally, from my discovery of the codes in Genesis 1.1–2, I already knew that the outer ring of 906 discs was the numerical equivalent of this pairing:

Jesus + Second Coming (s) = 906

The Creation Snowflake, then, is a frozen miracle, symbolizing God's immanence in Creation and proclaiming the return of our Lord Jesus Christ in a beautifully visual form. It reminds me of a Tibetan *mandala*, a circular representation of the sacred, used as an aid to meditation, or in Jungian psychology a visualization of the contents of the unconscious mind, used as an aid to psychoanalysis. Similarly, the Creation Snowflake is nothing less than a thought of God in visual form.

Here, then, are the six versions of the message brought to us by the Creation Snowflake, five of which are numerically equal to the snowflake (the sixth representing its outer ring), and all of which are equivalent in meaning (figure 30).

Figure 30 The Creation Snowflake as a *Mandala* symbolising The Second Coming

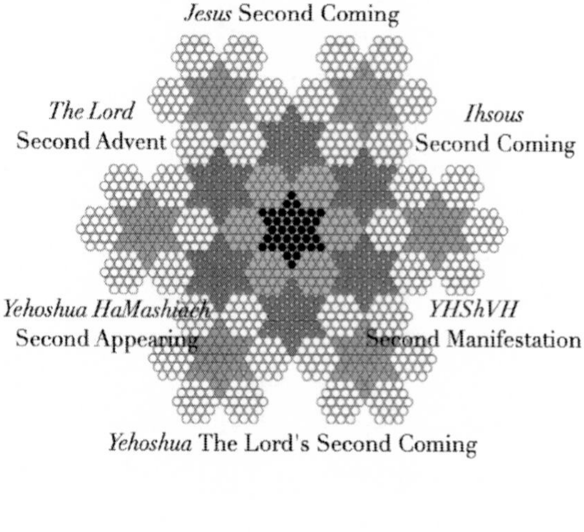

Jesus Second Coming

The Lord Second Advent

Ihsous Second Coming

Yehoshua HaMashiach Second Appearing

YHShVH Second Manifestation

Yehoshua The Lord's Second Coming

Chapter 11

Bisecting the Bible

And what rough beast, its hour come round at last,
Slouches towards Bethlehem to be born?
W. B. Yeats, 'The Second Coming'

There's a wonderful moment in William Tyler's 1959 production of *Ben-Hur*, which I think is a perfect reflection of the contemporary Christian image of Jesus Christ. After ben-Hur has been unjustly accused of trying to kill the Roman governor of Judea, he is led away in chains to the slave galleys. The party stop at a small village so that everyone can get a much-needed drink of water – everyone, that is, except ben-Hur, who has been singled out for particularly harsh treatment. In utter despair, he sinks to his knees and prays for God's help. Then he feels cool water pouring over his face and looks up to see a stranger leaning over him, offering him the refreshment he so desperately needs.

The stranger is of course Jesus of Nazareth, and the image of a kindly savior helping the weak and oppressed is one most Christians carry in their hearts. The idea that this same Jesus could have engineered the 9/11 attacks and shed the blood of three thousand innocent people – even though the Bible itself states in unequivocal terms that Jesus' return would involve great destruction – is inconceivable to many of his followers. Yet the World Trade Center and Pentagon were potent symbols of a financial empire whose hegemony over the earth has trapped billions in grinding poverty. The more I mulled it over, the more I could envisage that 9/11 might be something the world needed, just as badly as Judah ben-Hur needed that life-saving draught of water.

The great Irish poet W. B. Yeats caught the flavor of the event (and our times in general) in a vision he wove into his prescient, apocalyptic poem 'The Second Coming', the last two lines of which I quote at the start of this chapter.[22] That 9/11 was something the Christian world neither expected nor desired was neither here nor there, in my view. As a drama designed to capture the world's attention and shock it into wakefulness, it had been extremely successful. Of course, the world didn't literally end, but for the psyche of anyone raised to believe in the values of western materialism, and for the American psyche in particular, it was apocalyptic.

Instead of looking for meaning or redemption in the event, and despite increased church attendance and other hopeful signs, the USA reacted with rage, defiance and aggression. That was understandable, of course, but I wondered how many Americans realized that their nation's actions in the world often created the same rage and desire for vengeance in others. Michael Scheuer, first director of the CIA's bin Laden unit, and no friend of the man, wrote, in his recent book *Osama bin Laden*: 'Americans ought to understand that bin Laden and the Islamists are attacking the United States and its allies precisely because of the negative impact their government's actions have in the Muslim world.'[23]

Many took solace in conspiracy theories, spun by those convinced that Al Qaeda couldn't have pulled off such a huge operation on their own. Al Qaeda were either helped, or were just a cover for a sinister black operation, involving the CIA, Mossad, the Freemasons or the fabled Illuminati. Looking at some of the evidence researchers had gathered, such as footage of WTC 7 collapsing at free-fall velocity, WTC owner Larry Silverstein admitting that they 'pulled' (demolished) Tower 7 and the curious inefficiency of the air defences on that morning, I thought people had very good reason to be suspicious. But it was hard to see how their conclusions of a 'false flag' operation or even a Satanic sacrifice could gel with my own and I realised I would soon be drowning in a sea of confusion if I pursued the 'human conspiracy' angle for too long. How could both the 9/11 conspiracy theorists and I be correct?

A very timely dream clarified the situation for me: *I see a woman setting off for work one morning from her city apartment. The atmosphere is very workaday and quite pleasant. Then I see a huge, black spider in the air above her, spinning an enormous web across the entire street. The atmosphere becomes sinister and threatening, although the woman is quite unaware of the change. But in the sky above the spider I now see a second spider, even larger, spinning a web that covers the entire city. Both the woman and the first spider are unaware of it.* The dream suggested that humankind was indeed being manipulated in secret but also that there were *two* levels of planning. It wasn't clear if the dream was referring to 9/11 (although as always 9/11 was very much on my mind at the time) or at what level these conspiracies were being spun. But the dream reassured me that the findings of the '9/11 truthers' and my own did not have to be mutually exclusive.

It was quite possible that there were two distinct levels of planning for 9/11: one level the work of man, the other the work of God. I knew that the unusual phenomena I'd experienced - leading me to become a Christian and training me to find the September-11 Code - were spiritual in origin. I was also certain that the code itself could not have been the work of any human cabal. It was too ancient (the codes in Ezra were at least 1000 years old, probably much older), too perfectly woven and, most of all, proclaimed the very opposite of what the US and its allies would have us believe about 9/11. If God could weave miraculous coincidences into my life, then he could do so with anyone, including the writers of Scripture and the translators of the NIV Bible.

By the same reasoning, if God could insert a code into an event he could also control the event itself, second-guessing any plans made at the human level. There's a distinction made in Christian theology between *proximate* causes and *ultimate* causes. Whatever the immediate (proximate) causes of an event – whether a birth, a cyclone or a terrorist attack – ultimately God is in control. As far as I could determine, this same God was the creator of the September-11 Code. However, none of the many people who contributed to the development of the Bible would have had any idea they were being used to create this code. Neither would any of the prophets who wrote down their apocalyptic visions have known what future event they were recording. And no matter who the real players were in the 9/11 drama, the Stage Director was well clear of any human influence. In short, I was more interested in the message than in the details of how it was delivered, because ultimately it came from God.

* * *

As my comprehension of the code developed, I began to see that the entire Bible had somehow been put together with an eye on events that would take place on one single day in the remote future, within two faraway cities yet to be built on a continent unknown to the writers.

Daniel had a vision of a ram standing beside a canal, which 'did as he pleased and became great'. The ram had two long horns which were shattered when it was attacked by a goat with a single horn 'crossing the whole earth without touching the ground'. I counted the number of chapters to Daniel 8, where the vision is given, and found that it is the Bible's 858th chapter (11 x 78). The ram is described in verses 3 and 4, which have an ordinal value of 3102 (11 x 282). The destruction of the ram's horns is described in verses 5, 6 and 7, which have an ordinal value of 4555 (911 x 5). Considering that 9/11 took place almost 2500 years after that great prophet's time, this is an amazingly prescient vision, including an accurate description, in a preindustrial age, of an airplane.

The prophet Zechariah had a vision of four chariots, coming out from between two mountains:

> ^{1}I looked up again – and there before me were four chariots coming out from between two mountains – mountains of bronze! ^{2}The first chariot had red horses, the second black, ^{3}the third white, and the fourth dappled – all of them powerful.
> (Zechariah 6.1–3)

Verses four and five make it clear that these chariots have come from heaven:

> ^{4}I asked the angel who was speaking to me, 'What are these, my lord?' ^{5}The angel answered me, 'These are the four spirits of heaven, going out from standing in the presence of the LORD of the whole world.'(Zechariah 6.4–5)

This passage is marked with numbers that identify it as a prophecy of 9/11. Firstly, the conclusion of the passage is verse 8, which is tagged with the number eleven, as it is Zechariah's 77th verse, 77 also being the ordinal value of 'Christ'. The words of the verse indicate that the black horses have fulfilled God's purpose in the land of the north:

> 'Then he called to me, "Look, those going towards the north country have given my spirit rest in the land of the north"' (Zechariah 6.8).

Secondly, the ordinal value of this verse is the standard value of a phrase for the Second Coming:

> Then he called to me, 'Look, those going towards the north

country have given my spirit rest in the land of the north.' = 1146

The Second Coming of the Messiah (s) = 1146

Even the words and actions of Jesus in the Gospels repeatedly alluded to 9/11, a view the code confirmed for me.

In Matthew 21.12 Jesus enters the temple area, drives out the buyers and sellers, and overturns the tables of the money-changers. 2112 is 11 x 192 and the verse is the NIV Bible's 23,837th, 23,837 being 11 x 11 x 197. So the tables were overturned again on 9/11.

In Matthew 24.2, Jesus forewarns that the Jerusalem Temple will be destroyed. 242 is 11 x 11 x 2 and therefore another double multiple of eleven. The same warning from Jesus is given in Mark 13.2. 132 is 11 x 12. Luke's version is in Luke 21.6. 216 is 6 x 6 x 6.

Mark 11 describes Jesus' triumphal entry into Jerusalem (Mark 11.11) and also describes how he overturns the tables of the money-changers and makes a fig-tree wither. The withered fig-tree, an image of the fallen towers, is described in Mark 11.20; in the NIV, this verse has an ordinal value of 803 (11 x 73). Wondering why Mark 11 contained so much prophetic gold, I worked out its place value. It was the Bible's 968th chapter and 968 is 11 x 11 x 8.

In Luke 21.11, Jesus reveals to his disciples some of the signs of the 'end of the age'. 'There will be great earthquakes, famines and pestilences in various places, and fearful events and great signs from heaven.' In the NIV, the ordinal value of this, the eleventh verse, is 1111 (11 x 101).

In Luke 21.27, Jesus tells his disciples of his return. 'At that time they will see the Son of Man coming in a cloud with power and great glory'. The ordinal value here is 814 (11 x 74).

In John 9.11, Jesus rubs mud in the eyes of a blind man, after which his sight is restored. In the NIV, verse 11 has an ordinal value of 1298 (11 x 118) and John 9 is the New Testament's 77th chapter. Once we were blind but now we can see.

In John 13, the Bible's 1010th chapter, Jesus washes the feet of his disciples. The NIV version of the verse has an ordinal value of 1232 (11 x 112). The two feet stood for the twin towers, of which we were 'washed clean' on that terrible day.

* * *

Yeats saw the returning Messiah not as 'the Lamb', washing away the sins of the world through his blood, but as a 'rough beast' returning in a tidal wave of blood, which was certainly in line with Christian expectations of the Apocalypse and Christ's return. Many Christians believe that the Second Coming will be the literal return of Jesus Christ. Although I didn't rule it out I saw no reason to hold to that belief myself, because much of what most Christians take to be literal, I understand to be symbolic. However, since it was now clear to me that 9/11 announced Christ's return, I wondered if the man who engineered the event on the ground, Osama bin Laden, was associated with the 'rough beast' in any way.

As I wrote earlier, bin Laden's full name is linked to the word 'Messiah' through gematria:

Osama bin Muhammad bin Awad bin Laden (o) = 263
Messiah (s) = 263

Since the World Trade Center towers had been marked with the name 'Yeshua', I at first thought that the identification of bin Laden's name with 'Messiah' was just another example of a general link made between the players in the 9/11 production and the return of Jesus Christ. I later discovered that all of the versions of bin Laden's name had numerical values that suggested he had been born to fulfill his role as the engineer of the terrorist attacks on 9/11. For instance, as I showed, the two shorter versions of his name had ordinal values that were multiples of eleven (he was also 44 years of age on 9/11). Even more persuasively, the standard value of his full name held a numerical reference to the Messiah's Second Coming:

Osama bin Muhammad bin Awad bin Laden (s) = 1415
The Advent of the Messiah (s) = 1415

However, one numerical equivalence seemed to directly link him to the biblical Jesus, whose name was Yehoshua (here I am using the standard value of his Hebrew name, 391, which is one of the Signatures of Christ):

Osama bin Muhammad bin Awad bin Laden (s) = 1415
The Second Incarnation of Yehoshua (s) = 1415

Further clues to his possible identity kept turning up. For instance the name 'Osama' means 'lion', suggesting the Lion of Judah. He was born on 10 March, 1957, which meant he was 16,002 days old at the end of the second millennium and 16,256 days old on 9/11. These numbers are 254 x 63 and 254 x 64. Since 9/11 took place on the 254th day of the third millennium, both Osama bin Laden and the event he apparently masterminded were associated with this number, which is the ordinal value of this telling phrase:

Our Lord Jesus Christ (o) = 254

It is also linked with this word:

Risen (s) = 254

I wrote in chapter 6 that bin Laden, along with the World Trade

Center and the Pentagon, had the mark of the beast. How then could he be the Messiah? As I wrote in chapter 3, on the morning of 9/11 I awakened to hear the words 'Serpent power'. The serpent is of course associated with Satan, the serpent in the Garden of Eden. But in Exodus 7, Aaron, acting for Moses under the Lord's instruction, defeated Pharaoh's magicians by turning his staff into a snake:

> [10]So Moses and Aaron went to Pharaoh and did just as the LORD commanded. Aaron threw his staff down in front of Pharaoh and his officials, and it became a snake. [11]Pharaoh then summoned the wise men and sorcerers, and the Egyptian magicians also did the same things by their secret arts: [12]Each one threw down his staff and it became a snake. But Aaron's staff swallowed up their staffs.
> (Exodus 7.10–12)

These verses are streaked through with the number eleven, the number identifying 9/11-related encodings. Verse 10, where Aaron turns his staff into a snake, had an ordinal value of 1331, which is 11 x 11 x 11, a very rare triple multiple of eleven. The next verse is 11, and verse 12, where Aaron's staff-as-snake swallowed the other snakes, was the 165th in Exodus, 165 being 11 x 15. So this was yet another parable of 9/11. Moreover, the encoded elevens suggested something highly significant: *the 'serpent power' displayed on 9/11 was coming directly from the Lord.*

A connection between the divine and the serpent is implied in Hebrew gematria where the names the Serpent (*Ha Nachesh*) and the Messiah (*Ha Moshiach*) have the same numerical value, which is also a double multiple of eleven.

Ha Nachesh (s, Heb.) = 363 = 11 x 11 x 3
Ha Moshiach (s, Heb.) = 363 = 11 x 11 x 3

It was Aaron's staff that God turned into a snake and in chapter 7 I wrote about another staff belonging to Aaron that budded to show the Israelites that Aaron was God's chosen High Priest (and thus a forerunner of Christ, our High Priest). Aaron's staff that budded was one of the items Moses put in the Tabernacle and in chapter 7 I wrote that it represented the male organ. 9/11 – specifically, the three flights crashing into their targets – represented the act of physical union, as the High Priest entering the womb of the Most Holy Place. Since Osama bin Laden was the man held most responsible for 9/11, could he have been the High Priest?

Islam also expects a Second Coming of Jesus Christ and Jesus is expected to return as a Muslim or even to be an Imam (anointed leader, cleric or ruler). As these ideas went through my mind I continued to work on the code, awestruck at the possibility that the most hated man in the world was actually the redeemer of humankind.

> A lion has come out of his lair;
> a destroyer of nations has set out.
> He has left his place
> to lay waste your land.
> Your towns will lie in ruins
> without inhabitant.
> (Jeremiah 4.7)

This verse, Jeremiah's 88th, had an ordinal value of 1617 (11 x 147).

* * *

Most of the message carried by the NIV Bible was contained in the text, with additional information found in the chapter and verse indicators, place values, etc. However, it eventually occurred to me that perhaps the large-scale structure of the NIV Bible might contain additional information. I was led to this thought by some unusual features of the Bible. For instance the central chapter is Psalm 117 which is its shortest, with just two verses. Two verses later is Psalm 119, the Bible's longest, with 176 (11 x 16) verses.

The first task I set myself was to find out how many verses the NIV Bible contained. After consulting some websites and spending a laborious weekend double-checking the figures for myself, I confirmed that the NIV Bible has 31,086 verses. This seemed too good to be true, because I knew that the numbers 31 and 86 are the standard values of the Hebrew words *El*, meaning 'the Deity', and *Elohim*, meaning 'God' (the zero between them could be thought of as a kind of separator). The fact that two names of God were encoded again hinted at the Second Coming. Moreover, 31,086 is 11 x 2826, and so the NIV's verse count was also marked with the ubiquitous eleven.

However, what really piqued my interest was the other factor, 2826. The key had shown me two systems of letter substitution: ordinal values and standard values. I discovered a third system, reduced values, by myself, although I later learned that this was also a widely accepted substitution scheme (all three are used in the Kabbalah). I had long suspected, however, that the code used a fourth system of letter substitution. This was suggested to me by an incredible sequence of events that took place in 2003. I had joined a forum that discussed the '444' experiences many people around the world were having. Soon afterwards, I became friendly with one of the other forum users, a woman from the city of Atlanta, in the USA, named Cheryl Noland.

One day in June 2003, Cheryl and her daughter were sitting in a hospital waiting room when two hospital porters walked in, carrying a stretcher. This was an area the porters should not have been in, because there was little room for them and no reason to go there. The porters stopped beside my friend and her daughter, stared at them for a long time, then continued into an adjacent office. Cheryl said they had the words ANGEL RESCUE stitched into their uniforms. Her daughter said the words were GUARDIAN ANGEL TRANSPORT. The office the porters had entered had no other exit than the door they went through, but when her daughter, who by now knew something strange was going on, went to check on them she found that the office was empty. They now understood that these were no ordinary porters. They also said that on the way to the hospital they had noticed an unusual number of elevens on car registration plates, etc. Later, they discovered that two close friends of theirs had been killed in an accident that day.

Atlanta was a city I had never visited; in fact, I had never even been to the USA. Nor had I ever known anyone who had gone to Atlanta. However, two months later, two close work colleagues went to Atlanta on business. They were involved in an accident there, which hospitalized them both, an incredible parallel with the experience of my American friend, and verification that at least part of the message the angelic porters were delivering was for me. Intriguingly, the initial letters of the titles on the porters' uniforms (ARGAT) hinted at the word STARGATE, the New Age concept of a portal that allows entrance to a higher world (an idea also found in one of the films I thought resonated with 9/11: *2001: A Space Odyssey*). Not only that, but the words used 11 and 22 letters. All this suggested a possible link with 9/11 and the Second Coming.

I worked out the ordinal values of the two slightly tongue-in-cheek titles on the porters' uniforms:

Angel Rescue (o) = 110
Guardian Angel Transport (o) = 255

The number 110 was another obvious reference to 9/11, but 255 was even more interesting. It was the standard value of 'Lord

God'. However, it also happened to be the sum of the three number values I was using for the word 'Lord'.

Lord (s) = 184
Lord (o) = 49
Lord (r) = 22
184 + 49 + 22 = 255

Separating the phrase 'Guardian Angel Transport' into 'Guardian Angel' and 'Transport', I found that these had individual ordinal values of 114 and 141, which are the sums of the three number values of the word 'God' and the Hebrew word for God, 'Elohim'.

God (s) = 71
God (o) = 26
God (r) = 17
71 + 26 + 17 = 114

Elohim (s, Heb.) = 86
Elohim (o, Heb.) = 41
Elohim (r, Heb.) = 14
86 + 41 + 14 = 141

I realized that this might be a fourth system of numbering words for me to use and called it the *combined value*, although I was aware that there was no precedent for it. However, some unusual support for this idea came from a famous array of numbers known as Pascal's triangle, which has a multitude of applications in mathematics. The first eight rows of Pascal's triangle are shown in figure 31.

Figure 31 Pascal's Triangle - First Eight Rows

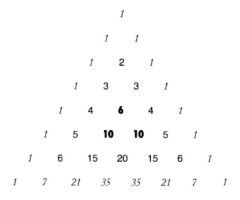

The sum of all the numbers here is 255, which I knew is the combined value of 'Lord'. However, I also found to my great surprise that the combined values of Elohim (141) and God (114) correspond to the outline of the triangle, shown by the italicised numbers(141) and the solid triangle within, shown by the non-italicised numbers(114). It didn't seem accidental that the English and Hebrew words for God were associated with such a celebrated object, known in China and India in Medieval times and studied by mathematicians to this day. If this correspondance really was deliberate then it had to be some kind of divine approval for the combined system of numeration.

I discovered several more connections between Pascal's triangle and the names of God, but I would just like to mention a couple more here. The three emboldened numbers at the very center of the array form a little triangle of 10, 6, and 10. These sum to 26, the ordinal value of 'God' and the standard/ordinal values of the personal name of God and most sacred word in Hebrew, 'YHVH' (Yod, He, Vav, He). The four Hebrew letters comprising YHVH have individual numerical values that almost perfectly reflect the three numbers at the center of the triangle, because Yod = 10, Vav = 6 and each He is 5, summing to 10. Compete perfection is found in the Hebrew letter Aleph, the 'father' of the Hebrew alphabet, associated with the mysteries of the Godhead and God's silent presence in our lives. This character is formed from two Yods and a Vav, and the numerical values of these constituents sit at the center of the nest of triangles (figure 32).

Figure 32 Aleph Within Pascal's Triangle

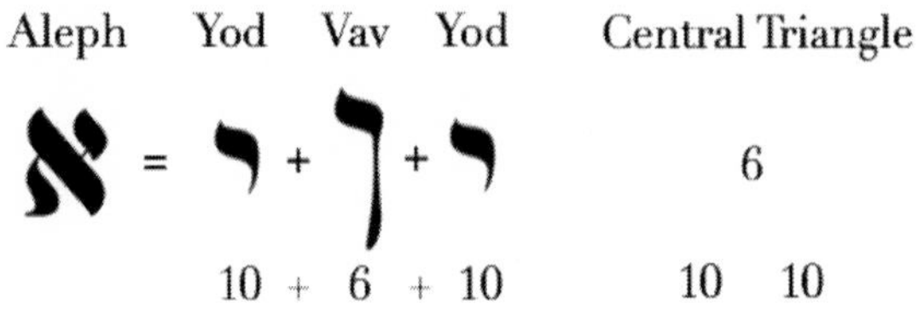

| Aleph | Yod | Vav | Yod | Central Triangle |

These fabulous connections appeared to be far beyond chance and to speak of a God who designs our languages to subtly reflect the universal language of mathematics.

* * *

It was when I worked out the combined values of some words and phrases for my database that I again came across the number 2826 (the factor of 31,086 that I mentioned earlier). It is the combined value of the following phrase:

The Second Coming of Our Lord Jesus Christ (c) = 2826

So the number of verses in the NIV Bible contained two Hebrew names for our Creator (El and Elohim) and was divisible by the key number 11, the other factor of 2826 summarizing the message of the code itself. This had to be by design.

Not long after I realized the importance of the number 2826, I found it in Ezra's list of returned exiles from Babylon, alongside the number 666. In chapter 6, I showed how a pattern of elevens is encoded into the first eighteen (6 + 6 + 6) names of the exiles, centered on the number 666 (see table 6.6 in chapter 6).

Since the encodings were focused on Ezra's counts, I summed the numbers of the exiles in rows 7, 9, 11, 13 and 15, which was where the encodings lay. To my astonishment, I found the combined values of three well-known phrases for the Second Coming (table 11.1).

Table 11.1 The Second Coming in Ezra				
Verse	Row	Count	R.T.	R.T. combined value of...
9	7	760	760	-
10	8	-	-	-
11	9	623	1383	The Lord's Second Appearing
12	10	-	-	-
13	11	666	2049	The Second Coming of Jesus Christ
14	12	-	-	-
15	13	454	2503	-
16	14	-	-	-
17	15	323	2826	The Second Coming of Our Lord Jesus Christ

Notice that the first two encodings are associated with the number 11, through the verse number and place value. This neat little pattern of three encodings ends with the Bezai in Ezra 2.17 and I found that the third encoding is also associated with eleven. Earlier I showed that 217 was encoded in the fall of the three WTC buildings, and is the ordinal value of 'Christ's Second Coming'. It so happens that Ezra 2.17 is the 12,045th verse in the NIV Bible, this being 11 x 1095. On top of that, the number 1095 is also associated with the Second Coming:

The Second Advent (s) = 1095

Finally, the Bezai are listed in verse 17 of Ezra 2 and verse 23 of Nehemiah 7. The numbers 17 and 23 multiply to give 391, the standard value of 'Second Coming'. I had stumbled upon another dazzling confluence of meaningfully related numbers within the NIV Bible.

Because 31,086 is an even number, there is no single central verse in the NIV Bible. Instead there are two middle verses, which are Psalm 102, verses 21 and 22. I knew that the first two and last two verses of the NIV Bible were encoded with numbers proclaiming the Second Coming. It occurred to me that these two middle verses might be similarly encoded. Here they are:

21 So the name of the LORD will be declared in Zion
and his praise in Jerusalem
22 when the peoples and the kingdoms
assemble to worship the LORD.
(Psalm 102.21–22)

I noticed that the two verses were actually one sentence, divided for convenience, and that they stood on their own as one statement. This was a good start. I read through the entire psalm, which is the prayer of an 'afflicted man' and I noticed that verses 21 and 22 are almost the only uplifting verses within it. In fact the verse immediately preceding them is quite somber: 'to hear the groans of the prisoners and release those condemned to death'. The verse after them is even darker: 'In the course of my life he broke my strength; he cut short my days.' So verses 21 and 22 appeared to me to have been deliberately positioned at the center of God's Word.

The encodings of the Second Coming in Genesis and Revelation covered the first and last eighteen words of the NIV Bible. My intuition told me there might be a similar pattern here, so I calculated the ordinal value (as usual) of the first eighteen words of Psalm 102.21–22:

So the name of the LORD will be declared in Zion and his praise in Jerusalem when the (o) = 738
The Second Appearing (s) = 738

By this stage I was beyond any doubts about the authenticity of the code, but this was thrilling confirmation that it was real, nonetheless. As I said, the last eighteen words of the NIV Bible were also encoded with the message of the Second Coming, so I numerated the last eighteen words of these two central verses to see if the same pattern held here:

in Zion and his praise in Jerusalem when the peoples and the kingdoms assemble to worship the LORD (o) = 953
Second Manifestation (s) = 953

Again the text was encoded with the message of the Second Coming! Looking to see what else might be dug up there, I found the name of the one whose return this magnificent piece of code proclaimed. It was buried within the central nineteen words of the two verses.

the LORD will be declared in Zion and his praise in Jerusalem when the peoples and the kingdoms assemble (o) = 925
Jesus Christ (s) = 925

So by the simple act of splitting the NIV Bible in two, I discovered two verses that encapsulated the entire code, like seeds in the center of a split melon (table 11.2). These beautiful encodings are summarized below.

Table 11.2 The Second Coming In Psalm 102				
So the name of	the Lord will be declared	in Zion and his praise in Jerusalem when the	peoples and the kingdoms assemble	to worship the Lord.
The Second Appearing				
	Jesus Christ			
		Second Manifestation		

In searching for larger-scale encodings within the NIV Bible I also found a kind of seal on the September-11 Code, revealed by simply joining the NIV's first and last verses.

In the beginning God created the heavens and the earth (o) = 430

The grace of the Lord Jesus be with God's people. Amen. (o) = 458

430 + 458 = 888

Ihsous (s, Gr.) = 888
The Lord's Second Coming (s) = 888

So the first and last verses of the NIV Bible joined together to create the seal of the Alpha and Omega himself.

I made the findings related to the 31,086 verses in the NIV Bible on the weekend of 7–8 November, 2009. I got unusual verification of the significance of this discovery through the Google logo on 11/9/09 (note the date), which I saw when I switched on my computer that day. The logo was written in numbers to celebrate the 40th anniversary of *Sesame Street* and was displayed in selected countries, including the UK. It featured Count von Count, who teaches children to count in *Sesame Street*, and the Google logo was written as the numbers 600813 (I can't reproduce the logo here).[24] Reading backwards, it can be seen that the digits of 31 and 86 are there in the correct order. I'm not saying that the sign was put there to show the world what I'd done, simply that my discovery was timed through synchronicity to coincide with the commemorative logo being put on the Google homepage. I believe it was done to impress upon me the significance of what I'd found.

* * *

Soon after discovering the systems of gematria I used, it occurred to me to numerate my own name, initially just for fun. The results were fascinating and more than a little alarming. Among many interesting numbers, I found that the standard value of my full name is 2112 (11 x 192), another example of my destiny being shown in my numbers. I had previously laughed inwardly at people who practiced numerology, which I found childish and implausible, but I was now in my own way a more committed numerologist than anyone else I knew.

The ordinal value of my full name is 240 and, because I thought of myself as a bit-part player in the end-times drama, I never expected to find it encoded in the NIV Bible. But I did find it. The first place it showed up was in Revelation 13.18, along with another number that showed this was no chance occurrence (table 11.3).

Table 11.3 The Author's Name in Revelation 13.18 (NIV)	
This calls for wisdom. If	anyone has insight, let him calculate the number of the beast, for it is man's number. His number is 666.
William Newton Downie	911

The second apparent encoding was even more fabulous. In chapter 5, I showed how I had found that the name 'God' was encoded within the first twenty-four letters of Genesis 1, with a skip of eight letters. After finding it I turned to the first book of the New Testament to see if anything was encoded there. What I found in this high-profile location, partly mirroring the Genesis encodings, was my full name encoded over three eight-letter strings, each string encoding one of my names (table 11.4).

Table 11.4 The Author's Name in Matthew 1.1 (NIV)		
ArecordofthegenealogyofJ		
8 letters	8 letters	8 letters
William		
William Downie		
William Newton Downie		

Like the Revelation encoding, the ordinal value of the rest of the verse, 429, prophesies my code work:

The Second Coming of our Lord Jesus Christ (o) = 429

I'm still stunned by this encoding as I write. Both encodings seem to imply that I was the person who was supposed to find the September-11 Code. If so, then it also explained something that had always troubled me. The NIV Bible I had was written in British English, whereas American readers would have the American English version. There was almost no difference between them as far as encoded material was concerned, apart from one passage which seemed to be encoded in the British English version but not in the American English version. That implied that the entire biblical part of the code was found not just in the 1984 edition of the NIV Bible but in the *British* English version. It made sense then that if I was the one meant to find the code, then the fully encoded text would be found in the version published in the UK.

Using the combined system I found more evidence linking Osama bin Laden with the figure of Jesus Christ:

Osama bin Muhammad bin Laden (c) = 1149
Our Lord Jesus (s) = 1149

Osama bin Muhammad bin Awad bin Laden (c) = 1797
Jesus the Messiah + Second Coming (c) = 1797

According to the book *Osama bin Laden*, by Michael Scheuer, first head of the CIA's bin Laden unit, and in contrast to the stories appearing in the media about Osama bin Laden, he was a pious man of high intelligence, gentle manners and great integrity, who was well liked and respected by those around him. Yet I found the idea that Jesus could have returned as a Muslim who wished to convert the world to Islam by violent Jihad difficult to accept, and clung on to the idea that Osama bin Laden had been unwittingly used to fulfill biblical prophecy. Perhaps, like those who wished to believe stories that bin Laden mistreated his family, had a drunken youth and was the rich dupe of other Muslim extremists, I was protecting myself from the unpalatable truth. If Jesus really had incarnated again as Osama bin Laden, it simply had to be accepted.

However, I had a feeling I didn't have the whole picture. This was partly because of the evidence I'd so far found. Much of it did suggest he was the Messiah and some of the biblical encodings of the Second Coming (such as the Sign of the Cross) included encodings of Osama bin Laden's name. However, the most significant piece of code I'd found, the striking pattern of encoded numbers in Genesis I called the Signatures of Christ, did not appear to have bin Laden's numerical signature. Another reason for my hesitation was my growing interest in another figure on the world stage.

Chapter 12

The Resurrection of Christ

Rise, let us go!
   Matthew 26.46

In my dreams and visions I occasionally saw myself approaching a door. I was always inside a building of some sort, often in gloom or darkness, but the world beyond the door was flooded with a golden light. My journey towards the door began about 2003, and, as the months and years progressed, I inched ever closer to it. I knew it was yet another representation of Christ, one which is well known to Christians: 'I am the door: by me if any man enter in, he shall be saved, and shall go in and out, and find pasture' (John 10.9, KJV). Then, on Good Friday, 2008, I finally got through – or some part of me at least. As I entered the golden realm in my mind a voice said to me: 'I'm lightly pleased that you've made it.' These words had an ordinal value of 366, the combined value of 'Messiah', so I knew who was addressing me. The pun 'lightly' for 'rightly' was a reference to God being 'the Light'.

For the next two days I felt different inside. My internal dialogue, usually negative and critical, was now positive and uplifting, and my dreams and visions were filled with light. I returned through the door on Easter Sunday, meaning I fell back to my usual state of consciousness. In fact I've been through that door several times, each time falling back within a few days or hours, because I eventually reverted to my old ways of thinking and acting. I don't know if it's possible to live here on earth and stay permanently on the other side of the door. For me, it has been difficult even to stay beyond the door for a little while. But

I know that it will always be waiting for me. My passing through the door seemed to be another fulfillment of the prophetic, multi-symbolic dream with which I began this book, except that the realm beyond the door was not an abyss to fall into, but a home to which we will all return, our final destination.

In a vision I had while driving I got a foretaste of this grand return. Feeling relaxed, I put on Steve Reich's *Variations for Wind, Strings and Keyboards*. Almost as soon as the music began I had the vision (somehow I could see the vision and the road ahead at the same time). *Hundreds of children are running up a gentle, grassy hill on a sunny day. At the top of the hill is the Heavenly Father, waiting to welcome them home. The children have been gone a long, long time, but are finally coming home, screaming with joy at their return. The air is filled with every emotion imaginable, yet underneath it all there is a feeling of absolute security, a sense that everything is really okay.*

* * *

By 2008 I thought I had found all the treasure there was to gather, but there was still one item to find – and this was the most dazzling jewel of all. As I worked on the September-11 Code, I was increasingly troubled by the fact that it was contained within the 66-book Protestant canon. The NIV itself was a Protestant version, created by a committee of scholars from many established Protestant traditions, but no representative of the Roman Catholic or Orthodox traditions. I knew that Roman Catholics made up about half of the world's Christians and Orthodox Christians about a quarter of the rest, so it seemed wrong to me that a huge swathe of the Christian community should be excluded from these revelations. By 2005, the only connections to Catholicism I had found were the eleventh Station of the Cross, depicting the nailing of Jesus to the Cross, and the fact that Pope John Paul II was the 264th Bishop of Rome, 264 being 11 x 24.

In December 2004, while I was catnapping, I heard the following words: 'You carry the baby's birth date.' Then, a little later, I heard 'Two thousand and five'. I knew, then, that something momentous was soon to occur. These words were also encoded with numbers. In particular, their ordinal value was 516, the standard value of 'The Appearing' and the combined value of 'the Lord'. In March 2005 I put up my webpage about the Creation Snowflake (see chapter 10). The impact of my work had been disappointing up until then, but this page made more of a splash and I was pleased with that. Many signs were given to me around then, so I also knew that whoever was guiding me was also pleased that I had made this find. I thought the predictions made in December 2004 had been fulfilled.

By March 2005, Pope John Paul II was gravely ill and it was thought that he might not live much longer. I am not a Roman Catholic, but I had begun to take an interest in the Pope, who was a most unusual man in many respects and a great ambassador for both Catholicism in particular and Christianity in general.

Karol Jozef Wojtyla became Pope on 16 October, 1978, after Pope John Paul I died unexpectedly. The new incumbent took the name John Paul II, in honor of his predecessor, and quickly became a major world leader, making pastoral visits to 129 countries and so becoming the most widely traveled pope in history. Among many achievements, John Paul II engendered a widespread renewal of Catholic Christian faith, particularly among young people, worked tirelessly to heal divisions between Christian communities and forged improved relations with other religions, particularly Judaism, Islam and Buddhism. He was credited with inspiring the collapse of communism in Eastern Europe but also regularly criticized the excesses of capitalism. Strong in faith and conservative in stance (although he supported Vatican II), this pope reached out to other faiths and Christian denominations in a way I found admirable, even if I didn't always agree with his traditionalist views.

A testament to John Paul II's character was his reaction after being shot four times by a would-be assassin, Mehmet Ali Agca, on 13 May, 1981 in St Peter's Square in Rome. He asked people to pray for Agca and later forgave him, meeting him in prison. This had a profound effect on Agca, and marked the beginning of a friendship with the Pope, who later met his mother and brother. After the Pope fell ill in 2005, Agca send him a letter wishing him a speedy recovery. John Paul II's attitude of forgiveness and reconciliation stands in marked contrast to the reaction of the USA and its allies after the 9/11 attacks. John Paul's forgiveness led to friendship. America's fury led to war.

This pope regularly drew enormous crowds. Five million worshippers were present at the papal gathering in Manila on 15 January, 1995, the largest such gathering in history. His funeral was a world-uniting event, possibly attracting the biggest TV audience in history. Four million mourners made pilgrimages to Vatican City during the memorial week that followed the funeral. Such was his impact that after his death many Catholic figures began referring to him as 'John Paul the Great'. He was only the fourth pope to have been so honored and the first pope since the first millennium. There were calls even at his funeral for him to be declared a saint and his beatification is now imminent.

The night after Pope John Paul II died I had the following dream: *I am standing with my wife outside our local cemetery. My old boss walks by with a determined look on his face. He has a large head but, as he passes, this turns into a white bishop's miter. My wife then says to me, 'That's our Lord lost his hands and his feet.'* On waking, I immediately understood that this dream was about Pope John Paul II. The cemetery symbolized death, of course. Catholic clergymen frequently make the Sign of the Cross and this particular pope traveled throughout the world to evangelize, which was what was meant by 'his hands and his feet'. I was disturbed by the fact that he was represented by my old boss (the one I had locked horns with), but I realized that my old boss was in the dream to represent authority and because he had a large head and white hair, which superficially resembled a miter. The fact that I had had such a difficult relationship with this man may also be a comment on how hard we resist spiritual authority. In the dream he was heading north, which in the dreamscape stands for the Source: he was returning to God.

A few days later, on 8 April, 2005, I saw the following words in my field of vision while I was taking a short catnap: 'I begin now.' This was the day of the Pope's funeral and I now realized that it was the moment I'd been told about in my vision in December 2004. I feverishly calculated the number of days that had elapsed since the turn of the millennium, which by now I knew had been used as the baseline for these end-time events. It was 1559 days, this number being the standard value of these words:

Our Lord Jesus Christ (s) = 1559

I already knew that 9/11 had occurred 254 days after the baseline, and that this was the ordinal value of the same words:

Our Lord Jesus Christ (o) = 254

These were of course the two systems on which the September-11 Code was built, so this was obviously a finding of the utmost significance: both 9/11 and the Pope's funeral bore the seal of our Lord. The words I had heard or seen on each of these days were similarly encoded:

Serpent power + I begin now (o) = 272
Jesus Christ + Second Coming (o) = 272

There were 1305 days between 9/11 and the Pope's funeral, which is slightly over three-and-a-half years, a period of time impressed upon us in various ways – three-and-a-half years (or days), forty-two months, 'time, times and half a time', 1260 days, 1290 days and 1335 days – in Daniel, Revelation and other prophetic books an important 'end times' marker. For instance:

> The man clothed in linen, who was above the waters of the river, lifted his right hand and his left hand towards heaven, and I heard him swear by him who lives for ever, saying, 'It will be for a time, times and half a time. When the power of the holy people has finally been broken all these things will be completed.' (Daniel 12.7, NIV) From the time that the daily sacrifice is abolished and the abomination that causes desolation is set up, there will be 1,290 days. Blessed is the one who waits for and reaches the end of the 1,335 days. (Daniel 12.11, NIV) The beast was given a mouth to utter proud words and blasphemies and to exercise his authority for forty-two months. (Revelation 13.5)

I wasn't sure how literally these prophecies should be taken, but this particular time period seemed to have been imprinted on the minds of these prophets, so I thought it was a good sign that there were three-and-a-half years between 9/11 and the Pope's funeral. Three-and-a-half years are just over 1278 days, which, counting from 9/11, would be the day before I put up my webpage on the Creation Snowflake, another good sign.

Another period of time is mentioned frequently in the Gospels, related this time to Jesus Christ: three days.

> 'Sir,' they said, 'we remember that while he was still alive that deceiver said, "After three days I will rise again."'(Matthew 27.63, NIV)

Jesus answered them, 'Destroy this temple, and I will raise it again in three days.' The Jews replied, 'It has taken forty-six years to build this temple, and you are going to raise it in three days?' But the temple he had spoken of was his body.

(John 2.19–21)

Since 9/11 symbolized the Crucifixion, it occurred to me that the three-and-a-half years between 9/11 and the Pope's funeral could have had the secondary purpose of symbolizing the three days between the Crucifixion and the miracle that took place on the third day. Was this the case, though? And what did this imply about the death and funeral of Pope John Paul II? I didn't know enough about either this particular pope or Catholicism to decide, so I began to gather more information.

What I discovered was that the Roman Catholic funeral liturgy is not really a memorial service for the deceased; it is focused solely on one person: Jesus Christ. *The Catechism of the Catholic Church* contains these statements on the meaning of death to Christians (the word 'Paschal' refers to the Paschal Lamb, Jesus Christ):[25]

1681 The Christian meaning of death is revealed in the light of the Paschal mystery of the death and resurrection of Christ, in whom resides our only hope. The Christian who dies in Christ Jesus is 'away from the body and at home with the Lord'.

1682 For the Christian the day of death inaugurates, at the end of his sacramental life, the fulfilment of his new birth begun at Baptism, the definitive 'conformity' to 'the image of the Son' conferred by the anointing of the Holy Spirit, and partici-pation in the feast of the Kingdom which was anticipated in the Eucharist – even if final purifications are still necessary for him in order to be clothed with the nuptial garment.

This was saying that the death of Christians is given meaning by the death and resurrection of Jesus Christ, to whose image they afterwards conform. That seemed to point to the funeral of Pope John Paul II having just the significance the code was implying. Moreover, the position of Pope is one of extraordinary significance to Catholics:

> The Bishop of Rome is the bishop of the Holy See and is more commonly referred to as the Pope ... Roman Catholic doctrine holds that the Bishop of Rome is the successor to the primacy of Simon Peter and thus the 'vicar of Christ' for the entire world.
>
> (Wikipedia)

So, for Catholics, the death of a pope was the death of Christ's representative on earth. Moreover, this particular pope was widely regarded as the greatest occupant of the Holy See in many centuries, perhaps of all time. Putting all this together, I made what could be the only possible conclusion: *for Roman Catholics, no event could have more fully symbolized the death and resurrection of Jesus Christ than the death and funeral of Pope John Paul II.*

My conclusion that the funeral of Pope John Paul II represented the Resurrection was supported by some very familiar numbers woven into the details of his life and papacy. For example, the ordinal value of his title, 'Pope John Paul II', was 151, just like 'Jesus Christ' and 'Holy Spirit'. The longer version, 'Pope John Paul the Second' had a value of 242 (11 x 11 x 2). I worked out the number of days from the birth of Karol Jozef Wojtyla (5/18/20) to the end of the second millennium, the primary reference date for the Second Coming's timetable: it was 29,447 (11 x 2677). The attempted assassination on 13 May, 1981 was 7172 (11 x 652) days before the end of the second millennium (which meant the Pope was 22,275, or 11 x 2025, days old). Next

I calculated how many days he had lived and was astonished to discover that it was exactly 31,000. This was something only one person in a thousand would manage, but on top of that, 31 is the standard value of the Hebrew root word for God, 'El', which made this particular number of days even more significant.

Sensing I was on the trail of something special, I worked out the standard values of the two most commonly used versions of his title and realized that this particular pope may have been very special indeed. I will simply give here the results I got and show where it is encoded within the NIV Bible (table 12.1).

Pope John Paul II (s) = 736
Pope John Paul the Second (s) = 1169

Table 12.1 Pope John Paul II Encoded Twice in Genesis		
In the beginning God created the heavens and (8 words)	the earth. Now the earth was formless and (8 words)	empty, darkness was over the surface of the (8 words)
Pope John Paul II		
	Yehoshua	
	Second Coming	
Pope John Paul the Second		

In a dazzling feat of alphanumerical virtuosity, the standard values of both versions of the title taken by this pope have somehow been inserted within the NIV Bible's first twenty-four words, right alongside the Signatures of Christ, the Creation Snowflake and the other encodings present there. This time, however, the twenty-four words are trisected into 8-8-8, suggesting 888 ('Ihsous' and 'The Lord's Second Coming'). The central eight words have an ordinal value of 391, which is of course the standard value of 'Yehoshua' and 'Second Coming'; this was also another example of 391 crossing 888, as in Amos 9 and 2 Chronicles 24.

As if to underline their importance, the numbers 736 and 1169 were also found in the key I was given: they are the ordinal values of the first fourteen and twenty-two words of the key, the two verses that miraculously appeared on my Alpha Course director's bookmark:

May God himself, the God of peace, sanctify you through and through. May your (o) = 736
Pope John Paul II (s) = 736

May God himself, the God of peace, sanctify you through and through. May your whole spirit, soul and body be kept blameless (o) = 1169
Pope John Paul the Second (s) = 1169

The death and funeral service of Pope John Paul II had been a major act in the riveting drama created to announce the Second Coming, symbolizing the death and resurrection of Jesus Christ and thus completing the larger Passion drama begun on 9/11. Were these encodings implying anything more? The encodings, although spectacular, were not enough to convince me that the Pope had been anything more than just another person who had unwittingly played a part, albeit a major one, in God's message to us. I needed more evidence. And more evidence was what I found.

The first sixteen words of the NIV Bible provided another piece of that evidence.

Pope John Paul II (s) = 736
The Incarnation (s) = 736

In fact, as my penultimate table shows, the standard values of the word 'Jesus' and the phrases 'Pope John Paul II' and 'The Incarnation' are inserted twice within the NIV Bible, yet again within its opening words (table 12.2).

Table 12.2 Pope John Paul II Encoded Twice in Genesis 1		
In the beginning God created the heavens and the earth. Now the (12 words)	earth was formless and (4 words)	empty, darkness was over the surface of the deep and the (11 words)
Jesus	Pope John Paul II/The Incarnation	
Pope John Paul II/The Incarnation	Jesus	

John Paul II had been born Karol Jozef Wojtyla. In 2008 I discovered a revealing phrase with standard value equal to that of his full name in English. Amazingly, this is also the standard value of his name in his native Polish (if the accented versions of certain letters are assigned the same value as the unaccented letter). The letters of the Polish alphabet are ordered differently from their English equivalents, so this had to be by design, making the impact of this numerical equivalence doubly powerful.

The Second Incarnation of Our Lord Jesus Christ (s) = 2583
Karol Jozef Wojtyla (s) = 2583

The jewel in the crown of my evidence, though, was this simple statement, the numerical value of which was equal to the Greek title meaning 'Lord Jesus Christ':

Karol Jozef Wojtyla is the Messiah (s) = 3168
Kurios Ihsous Christos (s, Gr.) = 3168

But I had already found that the code was pointing to Osama bin Laden as the Messiah:

The Second Incarnation of Yehoshua (s) = 1415
Osama bin Muhammad bin Awad bin Laden (s) = 1415

Messiah (s) = 263
Osama bin Muhammad bin Awad bin Laden (o) = 263

As I was completing this chapter, I made a devastating, last-minute find: the name 'Osama bin Muhammad bin Laden' enshrined within the holographic matrix that contained the Signatures of Christ, the Creation Snowflake, the Ark of the Testimony and Pope John Paul II. As usual, the name was represented by its standard value and again it was found as a reflective pair (figure 12.3).

Table 12.3 Osama bin Laden Encoded Twice in Gen. 1			
In the beginning God created the heavens and the earth. Now the (12 words)	earth was formless and empty, darkness (6 words)	was over the surface of the deep and the spirit of (11 words)	God was hovering over the waters. And God (8 words)
Jesus	Yehoshua	Osama bin Muhammad bin Laden	
Jesus	Osama bin Muhammad bin Laden		Yehoshua

So there now appeared to be *two* candidates for the returned Messiah – Osama bin Laden and Karol Jozef Wojtyla – and this greatly worried me. The systems of gematria which I had been shown by the key and other miraculous phenomena and which had unfailingly uncovered the greater miracle that is the September-11 Code had led me to a fork in the road. I didn't know which way to turn; it looked as if the code in the end had failed me, because I could see no way of distinguishing between these two figures.

But then I recalled a powerful dream I had been given near the beginning of my work on the code: *I see a man standing in a room. He is tall, brown-skinned, Arabic in appearance and wearing white. Then another man replaces him, standing in exactly the same place. He is smaller, light-skinned, round-headed and European but also wearing white. Then I see the following words: THIS IS JESUS.* At the time I didn't fully understand the dream, because the funeral of the Pope had still to take place, but now I could see that the dream was making the same incredible assertion as the code. Jesus Christ returned as two people: Osama bin Laden, the man responsible for the 9/11 attacks and the most wanted terrorist in the world, and Karol Jozef Wojtyla, the man who rose to become the first non-Italian pope for almost five hundred years and the greatest pope of modern times.

The numbers encoded into their names when I combined them said the same thing. Here are just four examples:

Osama bin Muhammad bin Awad bin Laden and Karol Jozef Wojtyla are the Messiah (s) = 4625 = 925 x 5
Jesus Christ (s) = 925

Osama bin Muhammad bin Awad bin Laden and Karol Jozef Wojtyla are the Messiah (c) = 5523 = 263 x 21
Messiah (s) = 263

Osama bin Laden + Pope John Paul II (s) = 1089 = 363 x 3
Ha Moshiach (s, Heb.) = 363

Osama bin Muhammad bin Awad bin Laden + Karol Jozef Wojtyla (c) = 4677 = 1559 x 3
Our Lord Jesus Christ (s) = 1559

The Gospels state that Jesus will come 'in clouds with great power and glory' (Mark 13.26). What better way to return than by destroying the twin pillars of our satanic economic system in a real-life drama depicting his crucifixion and fulfilling end-time prophecies, *and* as a spiritual leader revered throughout the world, whose death represented his resurrection? Who better to return as than two deeply religious men, one responsible for destroying the twin symbols of global capitalism, the other the spiritual leader of half the world's Christians? And how better to announce the event than within the most popular modern version of his book, in the form accepted by most of the rest of his church, written in the international language of choice?

The way the Second Coming has apparently manifested is not part of any of the various end-time theologies of which I am aware. But nearly all of them were going to be wrong anyway, so their endless proliferation and the huge disparities in their interpretations of prophecies shows little more than how easy it has been to misinterpret the Bible. This is why an interpretation from God of recent world events was necessary in the first place, *so we would recognize Christ's return when it finally manifested.*

If Jesus really did return in this way then that would mean he incarnated as a member of each of the three Abrahamic religions, and, at least in a general sense, fulfilled the messianic prophecies in each religion. Jesus' first incarnation fulfilled (at least for Christians) Jewish prophecies of the coming of a Messiah. His Second Coming as the most prominent leader in the Christian world (Christ appearing as his own vicar!) *and* as the man who 'flung down' Satan in front of the world, symbolically fulfilled Christian prophecies. In Islam, Jesus (known to Muslims as the prophet Isa) is expected to return as a pious follower of the Quran, which of course was Osama bin Laden's Holy Book. It seemed to me, therefore, that Christ had honored the messianic expectations of all three religions.

Christians, along with Jews and Muslims, believe that God has two complementary attributes: mercy and justice:

Righteousness and justice are the foundation of your throne; love and faithfulness go before you.(Psalm 89.14, NIV)

Justice always comes first, then mercy, a concept that is built into the very foundations of the Bible, with the Old Testament laying down God's laws for his people, and the New Testament showing God's love for his people. The pattern of the Second Coming was the same: first we saw God's justice on 9/11, dispensed by his 'serpent', Osama bin Laden; secondly, we saw the funeral of Pope John Paul II, whose life of service, ministry of outreach and forgiving, peace-loving character exemplified God's mercy.

Most Christian end-time prophecies prepared us for a general catastrophe with worldwide destruction, which has not so far occurred. Notwithstanding the possibility of further destruction to come, my guess is that the real apocalypse is internal. Alexander Solzhenitsyn once observed that 'the line dividing good and evil cuts through the heart of every human being'. The Gospels say something similar. Jesus said, 'For from within, out of men's hearts, come evil thoughts, sexual immorality, theft, murder, adultery ...' (Mark 7.21, NIV). But he also told us, '... the kingdom of God is within you' (Luke 17.21, NIV). The battle for our souls is being fought within ourselves, in the deepest recesses of our own minds – and the battle is between our ego's unquenchable desires and God's will for us. 9/11 was a symbol and demonstration of the 'crucifixion' of the worldly ego-mind that has to take place in us before we are ready to inherit the kingdom of God, and this feels like the end of the world for those who go through it.

In addition to returning as Karol Jozef Wojtyla and Osama bin Laden, Jesus was apparently the guiding hand behind the encoding of the NIV Bible, the planning, execution and encoding of 9/11, all the other recent signs and manifestations of the Second Coming and much else besides. This would have been achieved through the ministry of the Holy Spirit – the Spirit of Christ, if you like. My application of E. E. Brooks' revelations to 9/11 suggested that the Spirit is descending into this realm by planting his word or seed in our prepared minds, then growing within us and making us Christ-like - an event prophesied in the Bible as the birth of the manchild. This is *our* resurrection, which is what 9/11 prepared us for and the funeral of Pope John Paul II celebrated, and it is what the Second Coming is really all about.

'And we, who with unveiled faces all reflect the

Lord's glory, are being transformed into his likeness
with ever-increasing glory, which comes from the Lord,
who is the Spirit' (2 Corinthians 3.18).

* * *

In 2004, I was contacted by a man named Murray Ayers, who
told me that he regularly spoke with Jesus. I was skeptical about
his claims, but I kept in occasional contact with him. In 2007
Murray wrote to me to say that Jesus (or Jeshua, as he called
him), had a message for me. The message encouraged me in my
work on the code and included a beautiful last statement, which
I was told would be for me to interpret. This final sentence
turned out to be encoded with numbers that showed me
Murray's claims were in fact genuine. Murray passed away in
2010, but the words Jesus spoke through him for me are
preserved. Here is that final, poetic sentence, which bears the
same message as my 'light bulb' experiences, and which I hope
rings in your heart as it does in mine.

Honor God,
hold each other,
seek out the light beyond the veil of shadows
and rejoice at its arrival.

Amen.

Epilogue

Even at his funeral there were calls for John Paul II to be canonized (made a saint). The usual five-year waiting period was waived for this extraordinary man and the beatification process begun by his successor, Benedict XVI, on 9 May, 2005. He was beatified on 1 May, 2011, in a ceremony that was attended by over a million Catholics. Also present was French nun Marie Simon-Pierre who was apparently cured of Parkinson's disease after praying for his intercession. One more miracle is required for him to be eligible for sainthood.

1 May, 2011 is the most numerically significant date I have ever found. It was the 121st day of the year, 3773rd day of the third millennium (11 x 343), the 3519th day since 9/11 (391 x 9), the 2220th day since the Pope died, the 2214th day since his funeral (369 x 6) and the 33,220th day since Karol Jozef Wojtyla was born (11 x 151 x 20). 369 is the combined value of 'Lord God'. You know by now what all the other numbers mean.

The death of Osama bin Laden was announced that evening. He was killed just after 1:00 a.m. on 2 May, 2011, Pakistan time (just after 9:00 p.m. on 1 May, 2011 BST, or 8:00 p.m. GMT) by a US operation. This was further devastating confirmation that the seemingly unconnected lives of these men were linked by a thread of divine will that in the end drew them tightly together. The assassination of bin Laden and beatification of John Paul II were also types of crucifixion and resurrection, I noted.

The Second Coming isn't just about birth, death and resurrection either. Another sign was the wedding of Prince William of Wales and Kate Middleton, which took place just two days before John Paul II's beatification, on 29 April, 2011. As was recently pointed out to me by Kathryn LeCorre, the marriage can be viewed as a symbol of the return of the Bridegroom for his bride.

Acknowledgments

First of all, I would like to thank my agent Susan Mears, her colleague Joanna Crosse and John Hunt and his team at O-Books for their faith in my very controversial manuscript. In bringing this message to the world I very much appreciated the assistance of Brian Allan, the late Murray Ayers, Kathryn LeCorre, Diana Gallovich, Karen Gush, Vernon Jenkins, Peter Kent, Richard McGough, Felicity Murrie, Cheryl Noland, Malcolm Robinson, James Rowntree and Gary val Tenuta. I would also like to pay tribute to the works of the late E. W. Bullinger and E. E. Brooks.

Many other people helped me over the last ten years, as I struggled to bring these revelations to light. Some may be aware they did so, others may not, but I thank them all from the bottom of my heart.

Finally, I would like to thank my wife and family for their saintly patience, as, Bible in one hand, calculator in the other, I absorbed myself in this unusual quest.

Notes

1. *Holy Bible, New International Version*, International Bible Society, 1984.
2. Philologos Religious Online Books (October 2001). Available from: http://philologos.org/__eb-nis/ (accessed 2008-11).
3. Alice Deejay, 'Better Off Alone', ISBA Music Entertainment Inc., 1998. Positiva Records, Universal and Republic, 1999.
4. Philologos Religious Online Books (October 2001). Available from: http://philologos.org/__eb-nis/four.htm (accessed 2006-11).
5. The Alpha Course is run by the Holy Trinity Brompton Church, in London.
6. Wikipedia, September 11 Attacks (September 2011). Available from: http://en.wikipedia.org/wiki/September_11_attacks (accessed August 2011).
7. Philologos Religious Online Books (October 2001). Available from: http://philologos.org/__eb-nis/eleven.htm (accessed 2006-11).
8. B. Donahue, 'Hidden Meanings'. Available from: http://www.hiddenmeanings.com (accessed May 2011).
9. Wikipedia, September 11 Attacks (September 2011). Available from: http://en.wikipedia.org/wiki/September_11_attacks (accessed August 2011).
10. Wikipedia, September 11 Attacks (September 2011). Available from: http://en.wikipedia.org/wiki/September_11_attacks (accessed August 2011).
11. V. Jenkins, 'The Other Bible Code'. Available from: http://www.otherbiblecode.com (accessed 2002).
12. Philologos Religious Online Books (October 2001). Available from: http://philologos.org/__eb-nis/six.htm (accessed 2006-11).
13. http://members.cox.net/8thday/index.htm

14. Philologos Religious Online Books (October 2001). Available from: http://philologos.org/__eb-nis/nine.htm (accessed 2006-11).

15. Lighthouse Library International Brooks, E.E. (2005). Available from: http://www.lighthouselibrary.com/searchdb .php?what=author&searchfor=|BROOKS,%20E.%20E|&typ e=&show=titles&showitems= (accessed November 2010).

16. Lighthouse Library International Brooks, E.E. (2005). Available   from: http://www.lighthouselibrary.com/read.php? sel=554&searchfor=||BROOKS,%20E.%20E||&type=&what =author (accessed November 2010).

17. Cockney Rebel, 'Make Me Smile (Come Up and See Me)', EMI, 1975.

18. Julia Ward Howe, 'The Battle Hymn of the Republic', 1862.

19. 'Miracle, the Sacred White Buffalo' (1994). Available from: http://www.whitebuffalomiracle.homestead.com. (accessed 2004).

20. I have adapted the table from one at http://www.biblestudy .org.

21. For more snowflakes by Wilson Bentley, see http://snowflake bentley.com/

22. R. A. McGough, *The Bible Wheel: The Divine Seal and Capstone of God's Word* (1995). Available from: http://www.bible-wheel.com (accessed 2003).

23. W. B. Yeats, *The Collected Poems of W. B. Yeats*, Wordsworth Editions, 2000, p. 160.

24. Michael Scheuer, *Osama bin Laden*, Oxford University Press, 2011, p. 2.

25. See the logo at http://www.google.com/logos/sesame street.html.

26. CATECHISM OF THE CATHOLIC CHURCH – Latin text copyright © Libreria Editrice Vaticana, Citta del Vaticano, 1993.

Bibliography

Bullinger, E. W. *Number in Scripture: Its Supernatural Design and SpiritualSignificance.* Philologos.

Campbell, Joseph. *The Hero with a Thousand Faces.* Pantheon, 2008.

Catechism of the Catholic Church – Latin text copyright © Libreria Editrice Vaticana, Citta del Vaticano, 1993.

Drosnin, M. *The Bible Code.* Phoenix, 1997.

Ford, Arielle. *More Hot Chocolate for the Mystical Soul.* Thorsons, 1999.

Hardin, G. W. and Ingrams, J. *The Messengers.* Pocket Star, 1998.

Holy Bible, King James Version, 1611.

Holy Bible, New International Version. Hodder & Stoughton, 1984.

Jung, C. G. *The Archetypes and the Collective Unconscious.* Routledge, 1991.

Leet, Leonora. *The Secret Doctrine of the Kabbalah.* Inner Traditions, 1999.

Mandelbrot, Benoit. *Fractals: Form, Chance and Dimension.* W. H. Freeman, 1977.

Orwell, George. *Nineteen Eighty-Four.* Secker and Warburg, 1949.

Peake, Mervyn. *Titus Groan.* Eyre and Spottiswoode, 1946.

Peck, M. Scott. *The Road Less Travelled.* Touchstone, 1998.

Peck, M. Scott. *Further along the Road Less Travelled.* Touchstone, 1998.

Peck, M. Scott. *People of the Lie.* Arrow, 1990.

Peck, M. Scott. *In Search of Stones.* Pocket Books, 1997.

Peck, M. Scott, Von Waldner, Marilyn, Kay, Patricia. *What Return Can I Make?* Arrow 1990.

Scheuer, Michael. *Osama bin Laden.* Oxford University Press, 2011.

Yeats, W. B. *The Collected Poems of W. B. Yeats.* Wordsworth Editions, 2000.

AXIS MUNDI
BOOKS

Axis Mundi Books, provide the most revealing and coherent explorations and investigations of the world of hidden or forbidden knowledge. Take a fascinating journey into the realm of Esoteric Mysteries, Magic, Mysticism, Angels, Cosmology, Alchemy, Gnosticism, Theosophy, Kabbalah, Secret Societies and Religions, Symbolism, Quantum Theory, Apocalyptic Mythology, Holy Grail and Alternative Views of Mainstream Religion.